FROM POVERTY TO POWER

GEW INTELLIGENCE UNIT

FROM POVERTY TO POWER

CHINA'S ECONOMIC RISE AND AMERICA'S DECLINE

Hichem Karoui (Ed.)

Global East-West (London)

CONTENTS

CONTENTS

HISTORICAL CONTEXT OF CHINA'S ECONOMIC TRANSFORMATION

INTRODUCTION TO ECONOMIC REFORMS IN CHINA

The late 1970s marked a pivotal period in the annals of China's history as it witnessed the initiation of comprehensive economic reforms orchestrated by the visionary leader, Deng Xiaoping. This watershed moment was underpinned by a backdrop of economic stagnation and social upheaval following years of rigid adherence to Maoist principles. Deng Xiaoping, with his pragmatic approach, recognized the urgent need for transformative measures to revitalize the flagging Chinese economy and propel the nation onto a trajectory of unprecedented growth and development. The overarching goal of these reforms was twofold: to modernize the economy and enhance China's global standing while addressing the pervasive poverty and deprivation that afflicted vast swathes of the population. Deng's vision encompassed a multifaceted strategy that sought to dismantle the antiquated command economy, introduce market-oriented mechanisms, and leverage external engagement to foster technological advancements and knowledge transfer. In doing so, he aimed to unleash the latent potential of the Chinese populace and harness the country's abundant resources for collective prosperity. Moreover, Deng's emphasis on 'socialism with Chinese characteristics' delineated a nuanced path distinct from orthodox socialist doctrines, thereby creating a conducive environment for fostering entrepreneurship, innovation, and wealth creation. The pursuit of these objectives demanded a seismic shift in policy paradigms, institutional frameworks, and ideological precepts, signaling a departure from the dogmatism and insularity that pervaded China's erstwhile economic modus operandi. Consequently, the initial phase of these reforms set the stage for a momentous transformation that would reshape the global economic landscape and position China as a formidable player in the international arena.

Pre-Reform Chinese Economy

The Chinese economy prior to the economic reforms embarked upon by Deng Xiaoping in the late 1970s was characterized by centralized planning, state ownership of enterprises, and strict regulation of economic activities. Under Mao Zedong's leadership, China pursued a policy of self-reliance and emphasized heavy industry and agriculture through large-scale collectivization. While this period saw some notable achievements, such as infrastructure development and industrial growth, it also led to inefficiencies, scarcity, and stagnation in many sectors.

The pre-reform Chinese economy was marked by a lack of market mechanisms, price distortions, and limited international trade. State control over resources and production meant that enterprises operated within a framework of central planning, often resulting in excess capacity, suboptimal resource allocation, and bureaucratic inefficiencies. The rigid state control stifled entrepreneurship and innovation, leading to a dearth of incentives for productivity and quality improvement.

Moreover, the agricultural sector faced significant challenges under the commune system, with widespread inefficiencies and low productivity. The collectivization of farms and strict adherence to communal labor had adverse effects, leading to food shortages and hindered agricultural development. In addition, the lack of incentives for farmers to improve their output contributed to these challenges.

The pre-reform Chinese economy also struggled with technological backwardness and limited exposure to international trade and investment. The closed nature of the economy led to a lack of access to advanced technologies and managerial practices, hampering industrial modernization and competitiveness on the global stage. Simultaneously, limited engagement with the global economy resulted in isolation from international best practices and inhibited the potential for economic growth and development.

Overall, the pre-reform Chinese economy was characterized by centralized control, inefficiencies, limited innovation, and inadequate integration with the global economy. These conditions set the stage for the transformative changes that would unfold during the subsequent era of economic reforms initiated under Deng Xiaoping's leadership.

DENG XIAOPING'S OPEN DOOR POLICY

Deng Xiaoping's Open Door Policy, introduced in the late 1970s, marked a monumental shift in China's economic trajectory.

Embracing a pragmatic approach, Deng sought to modernize China by opening up its economy to foreign investment and promoting market-oriented reforms. This policy aimed to break away from the isolationist tendencies of the Mao era and propel China onto the global stage as a significant player in the world economy.

Central to Deng's Open Door Policy was the emphasis on attracting foreign capital and technology to revitalize China's industrial and technological base. Special Economic Zones (SEZs) were established along China's coastline to serve as experimental hubs for introducing capitalist practices and foreign investments. These zones were pivotal in demonstrating the benefits of integrating China into the global market and served as catalysts for economic growth and development.

Moreover, Deng Xiaoping's policy heralded a departure from the centrally planned economy, encouraging the decentralization of decision-making and granting greater autonomy to local governments and businesses. The Open Door Policy also facilitated the liberalization of trade, resulting in China's increased participation in international commerce and the gradual dismantling of trade barriers.

In addition to economic reforms, Deng's Open Door Policy had wider implications for diplomatic relations. By fostering cross-border collaborations and forging strategic alliances with leading global economies, China positioned itself as a key player in the international arena, thereby strengthening its geopolitical influence.

The sweeping transformation brought about by Deng Xiaoping's Open Door Policy laid the foundation for China's rapid economic ascent and laid the groundwork for the remarkable transformation that would unfold in subsequent years. By embracing a more open, market-oriented approach, China harnessed its potential to become a major powerhouse in the global economy, reshaping not only its own fate but also altering the course of global economic dynamics.

Transition Mechanisms: From Plan to Market

During the late 1970s and early 1980s, China underwent a significant shift from a centrally planned economy towards a more market-oriented economic system. This transition was integral to Deng Xiaoping's reform policies and marked a pivotal moment in China's economic history. The process of transitioning from a centrally planned economy to a market-based system involved intricate mechanisms and multifaceted challenges. Central to this transformation was the dismantling of rigid state controls and the introduction of elements of free-market principles.

One of the fundamental aspects of this transition was the restructuring of state-owned enterprises (SOEs) and the introduction of private enterprise into the economy. Previously, SOEs had been the primary drivers of economic activity, but under the new policies, they were gradually reformed to operate in a more commercial manner. This reform aimed to improve efficiency, increase competition, and reduce the burden on the state budget while also attracting foreign investment and expertise.

Another critical aspect of this transition was the liberalization of prices and the removal of subsidies. The government began phasing out price controls and introduced market-driven pricing mechanisms for various goods and services. This shift incentivized producers to respond to market demand and allowed for more efficient allocation of resources. Additionally, the reduction of subsidies led to a more sustainable fiscal framework, alleviating the strain on public finances and fostering a more dynamic economic environment.

Furthermore, the financial sector underwent substantial changes during this period. Reforms included the establishment of specialized banks and financial instruments to facilitate capital allocation, as well as efforts to develop a stock market and other capital markets. These initiatives aimed to diversify and modernize China's financial system, encourage private investment, and support the growth of a vibrant private sector.

The transition from a planned to a market-oriented economy also involved extensive legal and institutional reforms. New laws and regulations were enacted to protect property rights, enhance contract enforcement, and create a more transparent legal framework for business operations. Simultaneously, administrative barriers to entrepreneurship and trade were steadily dismantled, promoting greater flexibility and innovation within the economy.

Overall, the transition mechanisms from plan to market represented a complex and ambitious endeavor that fundamentally reshaped China's economic landscape. This transformative process set the stage for subsequent developments and laid the groundwork for China's remarkable economic ascent on the global stage.

Special Economic Zones and Their Impact

Special Economic Zones (SEZs) have played a pivotal role in China's economic transformation. These designated areas were established with the primary objective of attracting foreign investment, promoting export-oriented growth, and experimenting with market-oriented policies. The first SEZ was set up in Shenzhen in 1980, followed by others in places like Zhuhai, Shantou, Xiamen, and Hainan Province. These zones were characterized by offering tax incentives, streamlined regulations, and infrastructure development to incentivize both domestic and foreign businesses to set up operations. The impact of these SEZs has been significant. They served as incubators for testing new economic policies and practices, providing valuable insights into the potential benefits of liberalization and globalization. The success of SEZs in attracting foreign investment and integrating China into the global economy prompted the replication of similar models in other developing countries. Moreover, the economic prosperity witnessed within these zones also led to the gradual spillover of their benefits to surrounding regions, further fueling China's overall economic growth. Today, China's SEZs continue to remain vital catalysts for economic development, serving as hubs for technological innovation, trade, and investment. Their success has not only contributed to China's economic rise but has also inspired many countries to adopt similar strategies in their pursuit of economic progress.

Agricultural Reforms and Rural Development

China's economic transformation was not limited to urban areas and industrial sectors; it also profoundly impacted rural regions through agricultural reforms and rural development. The agricultural reforms initiated in the late 1970s aimed to modernize and liberalize the agricultural sector, which had long been stifled by collectivization and inefficient state planning. One of the most significant shifts was the introduction of the Household Responsibility System, which allowed individual households to contract land and sell their produce in the market. This pivotal policy change brought about a remarkable surge in agricultural productivity and laid the foundation for China's rural economic development. Furthermore, the government's investment in rural infrastructure, education, and healthcare played a crucial role in improving living standards and fostering rural prosperity. Through targeted poverty alleviation programs and initiatives to stimulate agricultural mechanization and technological advancements, China achieved remarkable progress in addressing rural poverty and boosting agricultural output. The successful integration of rural areas into the broader trajectory of economic growth contributed significantly to the overall transformation of China's economy. However, challenges such as land fragmentation, environmental sustainability, and income disparities continue to shape the complex landscape of rural development in China. As ongoing reforms and policies seek to address these challenges, the significance of rural development in sustaining China's economic growth and social stability cannot be overstated.

Industrial Policy and State-Owned Enterprises

The industrial policy of China has played a crucial role in its economic transformation. At the onset of economic reforms, state-owned enterprises (SOEs) were the pillars of the Chinese economy, with significant control over key industries. The government's industrial policies were geared towards boosting the development of these state-owned enterprises to drive economic growth and technological advancement. This approach involved strategic planning and resource allocation by the government to foster the growth and stability of the industrial sector. Recognizing the importance of industrialization, China focused on nurturing sectors such as manufacturing, energy, and heavy industry to lay the foundation for sustained economic development. The state-led industrial policies facilitated technology transfer, infrastructure development, and foreign direct investment to bolster the capabilities of state-owned enterprises.

However, as China progressed through its economic transformation, the role and functioning of state-owned enterprises underwent significant changes. In the face of globalization and market-oriented reforms, the inefficiencies and rigidities within SOEs became apparent. The government had to undertake measures to reform and modernize these enterprises to enhance their competitiveness and align them with global standards. This transition involved restructuring, corporatization, and introducing elements of market competition within the state-owned sector. Moreover, the government implemented policies to encourage innovation, improve governance, and enhance operational efficiency within SOEs.

While the state's influence remains pronounced in many sectors through large state-controlled enterprises, the landscape has also witnessed the emergence of dynamic private enterprises, joint ventures, and foreign-invested companies. This evolving mix of ownership and competition has injected vitality into the industrial landscape, fostering innovation, productivity, and healthy market competition. Furthermore, China's industrial policies have increasingly focused on promoting sustainable development, technological innovation, and high-end manufacturing to propel the country up the global value chain.

As China continues to navigate the complexities of balancing state-led initiatives with market forces, the role of industrial policy and the evolution of state-owned enterprises will remain central to shaping the country's economic trajectory and global influence. Understanding the intricate interplay between government intervention, market dynamics, and technological advancements within the industrial sphere is pivotal for grasping the multifaceted nature of China's economic model and its impact on the global economy.

Economic Liberalization: Challenges and Achievements

Economic liberalization in China has been a pivotal aspect of the nation's economic transformation. The shift from a centrally planned to a market-oriented economy brought forth a multitude of challenges alongside remarkable achievements. One of the primary challenges was the need to strike a balance between embracing free-market principles and maintaining social stability. As state-owned enterprises underwent restructuring, there were concerns regarding unemployment and potential social unrest. However, through strategic policies and targeted investment in infrastructure and social welfare programs, China effectively managed this transitional period, ensuring sustainable economic growth while mitigating adverse social impacts.

Furthermore, achieving price liberalization posed substantial hurdles. The transition from administered prices to market-determined prices required careful calibration to prevent inflation and market distortions. The improvement in the pricing mechanism was instrumental in reallocating resources efficiently within the economy.

Amidst these challenges, the achievements of economic liberalization in China are undeniable. Market reforms bolstered innovation and entrepreneurship, leading to the emergence of dynamic private enterprises that have become key drivers of economic growth. Accession to the World Trade Organization in 2001 marked a significant milestone, facilitating broader integration into the global economy and fostering export-led growth. This period also witnessed soaring levels of foreign direct investment, signaling increased confidence in China's business environment and potential returns.

The liberalization of capital markets, albeit gradual, has enabled greater access to financing and investments, further invigorating the economy. Chinese companies gained opportunities to raise funds globally, while foreign investors could participate in China's burgeoning capital markets. Simultaneously, the banking sector underwent substantial reforms to enhance efficiency, risk management, and service quality. The liberalization of the financial sector has nurtured a more diverse and robust financial ecosystem, offering a spectrum of financial products and services catering to different segments of society.

This chapter delves into the complex interplay between challenges and achievements during China's economic liberalization, illustrating the nation's unwavering commitment to reform and development amidst a rapidly evolving global landscape.

Role of Subsequent Leaders in Continuing Economic Reforms

Following Deng Xiaoping, subsequent leaders played crucial roles in steering China's economic reforms and maintaining its momentum. Jiang Zemin's tenure marked the emphasis on technological advancement and modernization, with policies promoting innovation, entrepreneurship, and participation in global trade. His leadership also saw substantial efforts in privatizing state-owned enterprises and reorganizing key industries, laying the groundwork for a more market-oriented economy. The era under Jiang Zemin witnessed China's accession to the World Trade Organization, signaling a deeper integration into the global economy and opening new avenues for international trade and investment. Hu Jintao succeeded Jiang Zemin and focused on sustainable development, energy conservation, and environmental protection. Under his administration, there was an increasing alignment of economic policies with social welfare, addressing disparities and ensuring inclusive growth. Notably, Hu Jintao's leadership saw heightened investments in infrastructure and healthcare, further bolstering the foundation for sustained economic progress. Xi Jinping, the current President of China, has placed significant emphasis on structural reforms, technological innovation, and the transition towards high-quality development. His leadership has been characterized by initiatives to tackle corruption, deepen financial reforms, and enhance regulatory mechanisms to ensure a fair and competitive market environment. Additionally, Xi Jinping's vision includes the ambitious Belt and Road Initiative, aimed at fostering economic connectivity and cooperation across continents. Within this context, subsequent Chinese leaders have not only continued but evolved the economic reforms initiated by Deng Xiaoping, each contributing distinctively to the nation's economic trajectory, shaping China into a formidable global economic powerhouse.

Summary - The Great Poverty Reduction

The role of subsequent leaders in continuing economic reforms has been pivotal in shaping the trajectory of China's economic transformation. The transition from traditional planned economy to market-driven approach was not without challenges, and it required perseverance and astute policy decisions from leadership across successive administrations. As we delve into the next chapter, 'The Great Poverty Reduction,' it is crucial to understand the groundwork laid by these leaders and their enduring impact on the socio-economic landscape of China.

The great poverty reduction in China is a testament to the success of the nation's economic reforms. Following the initial stages of liberalization, China witnessed a remarkable decline in poverty levels, lifting millions out of impoverishment. Understanding the mechanisms driving this reduction is essential to comprehending the broader implications of China's economic model. From targeted development policies to investments in rural infrastructure and social welfare programs, the strategies employed in eradicating poverty serve as a beacon for other developing nations.

Moreover, delving into the great poverty reduction allows us to explore the multidimensional components of well-being beyond income measures. Health outcomes, access to education, and inclusive growth are integral facets that merit thorough examination. By addressing these aspects, the next chapter aims to illustrate the comprehensive nature of poverty reduction efforts and their resonance with the overarching theme of sustainable development.

Furthermore, analyzing the success story of poverty reduction in China paves the way for critical discussions on international cooperation and knowledge exchange. The lessons learned from China's endeavors can inform global anti-poverty initiatives, laying the groundwork for collaborative solutions to address economic disparity in various parts of the world. This transition sets the stage for a deeper exploration of the interplay between economic policies, societal progress, and global development agendas, thereby framing the discourse within a holistic paradigm.

As we embark on this insightful journey through China's economic evolution, it becomes evident that the narrative extends far beyond statistical prosperity or nominal indicators. It encapsulates a profound narrative of resilience, adaptability, and collective empowerment. The great poverty reduction signifies a defining chapter in China's economic story, embodying the spirit of progress and the pursuit of inclusive prosperity.

THE GREAT POVERTY REDUCTION

OVERVIEW OF POVERTY REDUCTION IN CHINA

China's remarkable journey in reducing poverty on an unprecedented scale has garnered global attention and admiration. With its sheer size and population, the magnitude of China's poverty alleviation efforts holds significant importance not only for the nation itself but also as a case study for developing economies worldwide. Over the past few decades, China has achieved an extraordinary feat by lifting over 800 million people out of poverty, reshaping the lives and destinies of millions of families. This mass-scale endeavor underscores the pivotal role that poverty reduction plays in the overarching narrative of the Chinese economic miracle. The interconnectedness between poverty reduction and broader economic development in China has been a cornerstone of national policy, showcasing a deep-rooted commitment to social welfare and human prosperity. As we delve deeper into this critical exploration, it becomes evident that the impact of poverty reduction extends beyond mere statistics – it is a reflection of socio-economic transformation, a testament to resilience, and a beacon of hope for countless individuals striving for a better future.

Defining Poverty: Metrics and Thresholds

Poverty, as a concept, is multi-dimensional, involving not only income insufficiency but also limited access to basic human needs such as food, shelter, healthcare, education, and more. This section delves into the multifaceted nature of poverty, exploring the various metrics and thresholds used to define and measure it. In contemporary economic discourse, poverty is commonly measured using income-based thresholds, where individuals or households earning below a certain level are categorized as living in poverty. However, this singular approach fails to encapsulate the full extent of deprivation experienced by those in need. As such, poverty measurement has evolved to encompass a broader set of indicators, including but not limited to access to education, healthcare, sanitation, and nutrition. Recognizing the limitations of traditional monetary measures, many researchers and policy-makers have adopted multidimensional poverty indices, which provide a more holistic view of people's well-being. These indices capture information regarding living standards, health, education, and social inclusion to present a comprehensive picture of poverty. Moreover, regional disparities and differences in cost of living are significant factors that must be considered when establishing poverty thresholds. A dollar might stretch further in rural areas compared to urban centers, altering the lived experience of poverty. Hence, adjusting poverty lines to reflect these variations is crucial for ensuring accurate assessments. Addressing poverty necessitates a nuanced understanding of its causes and manifestations, which vary across cultures and societies. By acknowledging the intricacies within poverty definitions, policy-makers can better tailor interventions to meet the diverse needs of their populations. The next subsection will delve into the statistical analysis of poverty trends and numbers, providing quantitative insights into China's remarkable trajectory in tackling poverty.

Statistical Analysis: Trends and Numbers

In examining the remarkable success of China's poverty reduction efforts, a comprehensive statistical analysis is imperative to gain insights into the trends and numbers that underpin this profound socio-economic transformation. Over the past few decades, China has witnessed unprecedented progress in eradicating poverty. By meticulously delving into the statistical data, we can discern the magnitude of this monumental shift. The statistical analysis reveals staggering figures depicting the substantial decline in the percentage of people living below the poverty line, unequivocally showcasing the efficacy of China's poverty alleviation strategies. Furthermore, these statistical insights elucidate the nuanced dynamics of poverty reduction across diverse regions and demographic segments within China. It allows us to unravel the underlying patterns and disparities, shedding light on the differential impact of anti-poverty measures on various strata of society. Examining the trends over time enables an assessment of the pace and trajectory of poverty reduction, providing valuable perspectives on the sustained commitment and evolving strategies in combating poverty. By dissecting the numbers, we can discern the correlation between economic growth, social development, and poverty reduction, illuminating the interconnectedness of these crucial factors. Moreover, statistical analyses serve as a robust foundation for evaluating the effectiveness and efficiency of specific poverty alleviation programs, offering constructive insights for ongoing refinement and optimization. The holistic approach to statistical analysis augments our understanding of the multifaceted nature of poverty reduction, serving as a compass for shaping future policies and initiatives aimed at fostering inclusive prosperity. As we navigate through the labyrinth of statistics, it becomes abundantly clear that while significant milestones have been achieved, there are still pockets of persistent poverty that necessitate targeted interventions. This information not only underscores the need for continued vigilance and concerted action but also accentuates the imperative of leveraging data-driven strategies to deliver impactful outcomes in the pursuit of sustainable development.

China's poverty reduction efforts have been marked by significant statistical achievements, reflecting the country's profound socio-economic transformation over the past few decades. Here are some key statistics and insights:

Absolute Poverty Reduction

1. **Number of People Lifted Out of Poverty**:
- Since 1980, China has lifted nearly 800 million people out of poverty, accounting for more than 75% of global poverty reduction during this period[1][4].
- The number of people living below the international poverty line of $1.90 per day fell from 84% in 1981 to below 0.5% by 2018[1][4].
2. **Rural Poverty**:
- China's rural poverty population decreased from 250 million in 1978 to 28.2 million in 2002, an 88.7% reduction[5].

- By 2020, China officially eradicated extreme rural poverty, with the poverty rate dropping to below 0.5%[1][3].

Relative Poverty Reduction

1. **Relative Poverty Rates**:
- Relative poverty, defined as half of mean income, was reduced from 85.2% to 41.0% between 1981 and 2008[3].
- The shift to measuring relative poverty will likely increase the nominal poverty rate, reflecting a more comprehensive understanding of poverty beyond mere subsistence levels[3].

Economic Growth and Poverty Reduction

1. **Economic Growth**:
- China's GDP per capita grew at an average rate of 8.1% from 1978 to 2002, significantly outpacing global averages[5].
- The first decade of reform saw rapid income gains in agriculture, followed by industrial growth in urban and rural areas, and later, the dynamism of export-oriented coastal areas spreading inland[1].
2. **Public Infrastructure Investments**:
- Sustained public investments in infrastructure, such as transportation, energy, and telecommunications, have been crucial in integrating rural areas with urban economies and enhancing overall productivity[1][4].

Regional and Demographic Disparities

1. **Urban-Rural Divide**:
   - While rural areas saw significant poverty reduction, urban areas also benefited from rural-to-urban migration, which helped reduce relative poverty but increased urban inequality[3].
   - The Western Development Strategy and other targeted interventions helped spread economic benefits to less developed regions[1].
2. **Social Policies**:
   - The expansion of social policies, including place-based interventions and the creation of a basic safety net for the rural population, played a crucial role in the later stages of poverty reduction[1][4].

Future Challenges and Policies

1. **Sustaining Gains**:
   - To sustain poverty reduction gains, China aims to focus on rural revitalization, improving social protection, and addressing relative poverty[4].
   - The transition towards a low-carbon growth model and the need for better social protection for migrant workers are key areas of focus[4].

In summary, the statistical analysis of China's poverty reduction efforts reveals a remarkable decline in poverty rates, driven by sustained economic growth, targeted social policies, and significant public infrastructure investments. However, challenges remain in addressing relative poverty and ensuring equitable growth across all regions and demographic segments.

Citations:
[1] https://www.brookings.edu/articles/whats-next-for-poverty-reduction-policies-in-china/
[2] https://www.undp.org/sites/g/files/zskgke326/files/migration/cn/UNDP-CH-PR.-Publications-Measuring-Poverty-with-Big-Data-in-China-reduced.pdf
[3] https://webapps.ilo.org/static/english/intserv/working-papers/wp023/index.html
[4] https://www.worldbank.org/en/news/press-release/2022/04/01/lifting-800-million-people-out-of-poverty-new-report-looks-at-lessons-from-china-s-experience
[5] https://www.imf.org/external/np/apd/seminars/2003/newdelhi/angang.pdf

Government Policies Driving Poverty Alleviation

China's remarkable success in poverty reduction can be attributed to a series of well-crafted government policies and initiatives aimed at uplifting the lives of its citizens. The government has been proactive in addressing the multifaceted nature of poverty, recognizing that sustainable change requires a comprehensive approach. One of the pivotal policies is the establishment of targeted poverty alleviation programs that prioritize the most vulnerable regions and populations. Through these programs, financial resources, infrastructure development, and social services are directed to areas with the highest poverty rates, ensuring that those in dire need receive the necessary support. This targeted approach reflects the government's commitment to addressing poverty at its roots and creating lasting impact. Moreover, the government has implemented measures to promote inclusive growth, empowering marginalized communities and fostering an environment conducive to socioeconomic advancement. This includes initiatives to facilitate access to credit and financial services for small-scale entrepreneurs, as well as support for vocational training and skill development. Additionally, the government's focus on job creation and labor market reforms has played a vital role in lifting individuals and families out of poverty. By bolstering employment opportunities and ensuring fair labor practices, the government has contributed to the economic empowerment of its citizens. Furthermore, China's social welfare system has undergone significant expansion, providing a safety net for those facing economic hardship. Efforts to enhance healthcare coverage, pension schemes, and social assistance programs have contributed to mitigating the impact of poverty and fostering greater resilience within communities. The government's commitment to equitable access to education has also been instrumental in combating poverty. By investing in educational infrastructure and promoting enrollment, particularly in rural areas, China has sought to break the cycle of intergenerational poverty and equip future generations with the tools for success. Overall, the coordinated efforts of the government, spanning various sectors and domains, underscore its dedication to driving meaningful and sustainable poverty alleviation.

Rural Reforms and Agricultural Advancements

Rural reforms and advancements in the agricultural sector have played a pivotal role in China's extraordinary poverty reduction efforts. The transformation of rural areas through policy reforms, technological advancements, and infrastructural improvements has significantly contributed to uplifting millions out of poverty. Historically, China's rural population faced challenges such as limited access to modern farming techniques, land fragmentation, and inadequate support systems. Addressing these issues required comprehensive reform strategies that brought about substantial changes.

One of the key initiatives was the establishment of collectivized farming known as the Household Responsibility System (HRS) in the late 1970s. This shift from communal farming to individual household responsibility led to a remarkable increase in agricultural productivity and income. Furthermore, the government's investment in rural infrastructure, irrigation systems, and agricultural research and development bolstered the sector's efficiency and output. These interventions not only elevated the living standards of rural inhabitants but also fostered economic growth at a national level.

Agricultural advancements have been paramount in modernizing farming practices. The integration of technology, such as precision agriculture, biotechnology, and IoT applications, has enhanced productivity and sustainability. Moreover, the adoption of eco-friendly practices and organic farming methods aligns with global trends and promotes environmental conservation. The dissemination of knowledge through agricultural extension programs and cooperatives has empowered farmers with the latest techniques and best practices, thereby improving their livelihoods and contributing to poverty reduction.

Additionally, the government's focus on rural development goes beyond agriculture. Initiatives promoting rural entrepreneurship, skill development, and diversification of rural economies have created alternative avenues for income generation. The encouragement of agro-industrialization and value addition activities has not only increased the economic resilience of rural communities but also positioned them as key contributors to the overall economic prosperity of the nation.

However, challenges persist, particularly in remote and underdeveloped regions. Issues such as uneven access to resources, market volatility, and environmental degradation necessitate continued attention and tailored solutions. Despite these challenges, the transformative impact of rural reforms and agricultural advancements underscores their significance in addressing poverty and fostering inclusive growth across China's diverse rural landscape.

Urbanization as a Tool for Economic Upliftment

Urbanization plays a pivotal role in uplifting economies by generating new opportunities and reshaping the socio-economic landscape. In the context of China's economic transformation, urbanization has been a significant driver of growth and poverty reduction. As rural populations migrate to urban centers in search of better livelihoods, they contribute to the swelling urban workforce, thereby fueling industrialization and productivity.

The process of urbanization fosters structural changes in the economy, leading to increased specialization and efficiency gains. Urban areas serve as hubs for innovation, entrepreneurship, and technological advancements, creating a conducive environment for private sector development and investment. Moreover, the concentration of diverse skill sets and knowledge in cities promotes knowledge spillovers and fosters a culture of continuous learning and improvement.

In the Chinese context, urbanization has led to the emergence of vibrant metropolitan centers that act as catalysts for economic growth. These cities attract multinational corporations, foster robust financial markets, and propel infrastructure development, thereby creating a favorable ecosystem for business expansion and trade. Furthermore, the rapid urbanization has given rise to a burgeoning consumer class, driving domestic demand and contributing to the overall expansion of the economy.

However, while urbanization brings about numerous opportunities, it also presents challenges that necessitate strategic planning and policy interventions. Managing the influx of migrants into urban areas requires adept urban planning to ensure sustainable development, adequate housing, and provision of essential services such as education, healthcare, and sanitation. Additionally, addressing environmental concerns and mitigating urban sprawl is imperative to sustain the long-term benefits of urbanization.

It is important to note that urbanization must be accompanied by measures to bridge the rural-urban divide and ensure inclusive growth. Policies focusing on enhancing rural infrastructure, promoting agribusiness, and providing access to education and healthcare in rural areas are integral for balanced economic development. Furthermore, initiatives aimed at developing small and medium-sized urban centers can distribute the benefits of urbanization across a wider geographic area.

In conclusion, urbanization stands as a powerful instrument for economic upliftment, driving productivity, innovation, and consumption. When managed effectively, it can spur inclusive and sustainable growth, propelling nations towards achieving their development objectives.

Education Initiatives for Sustainable Development

Education is a fundamental pillar for sustainable development and poverty reduction in any society, and China's initiatives in this field have been pivotal in driving its economic transformation. The Chinese government has prioritized education as a key tool for fostering social mobility and empowering individuals to contribute actively to the nation's growth. With significant investments in educational infrastructure and reforms, China has made commendable progress in expanding access to quality education across urban and rural areas. The country has focused on not only increasing enrollment rates but also improving the overall standard of education to equip its citizens with the necessary skills for a rapidly evolving economy. China's commitment to enhancing educational opportunities has been underscored by the implementation of various policies aimed at promoting school attendance, reducing dropout rates, and enhancing the proficiency of educators. Efforts to bridge the urban-rural education gap have yielded positive outcomes, contributing to a more equitable distribution of knowledge and resources. Additionally, the promotion of vocational and technical education has played a significant role in addressing labor market demands and enhancing the employability of the workforce. Furthermore, the integration of modern teaching methods and innovative technologies into the education system has set the stage for a more dynamic and interactive learning experience, aligning students with the demands of a globalized, knowledge-based economy. Notably, the emphasis on holistic development, incorporating moral and civic education alongside academic curriculum, reflects China's long-term vision for nurturing responsible, well-rounded individuals who can actively participate in the country's development goals. Through these comprehensive education initiatives, China is not only preparing its citizens for meaningful employment but also cultivating a knowledgeable and innovative workforce that can contribute to the sustainable development of the nation. As China continues to prioritize education as a cornerstone of its developmental agenda, the positive impact of these initiatives is expected to resonate across diverse sectors, forming an essential component of China's concerted efforts towards achieving sustainable prosperity and fostering social harmony.

Healthcare Improvements and Accessibility

Healthcare improvements and accessibility have been integral to China's remarkable transformation, particularly in combating poverty and enhancing the overall well-being of its citizens. The healthcare sector has seen significant advancements propelled by strategic policy reforms, increased investments, and a focus on expanding access to quality medical services. One key development has been the establishment of a universal healthcare system aimed at providing essential medical coverage to all Chinese citizens. This initiative has led to an expansion of health insurance coverage and improved access to primary care services, thereby reducing financial barriers to seeking medical assistance. Additionally, the government has prioritized infrastructure development, equipping rural areas with healthcare facilities and medical resources to bridge the urban-rural healthcare divide. Furthermore, China's efforts in healthcare innovation and research have resulted in breakthroughs in medical technology and pharmaceuticals, contributing to improved treatment options and disease management. Collaborations with international organizations and institutions have played a pivotal role in knowledge exchange, capacity building, and resource mobilization for healthcare initiatives. China's active engagement in global health partnerships has not only benefitted its own healthcare landscape but has also allowed for valuable contributions to international health agendas. Despite these strides, challenges persist, including disparities in healthcare access between regions and socioeconomic groups, as well as concerns regarding healthcare quality and patient safety. Addressing these issues will require continued policy focus, sustained investments, and ongoing collaboration between public and private stakeholders. Through a comprehensive approach to healthcare improvements and accessibility, China is paving the way for a healthier and more resilient society, thereby reinforcing the foundation for sustainable development and poverty reduction.

International Aid and Collaborations

International aid and collaborations have played a pivotal role in supporting China's poverty reduction initiatives. As China endeavors to tackle the multi-faceted challenges of poverty, partnerships with international organizations and foreign governments have been instrumental in enhancing the breadth and effectiveness of its poverty alleviation programs. These collaborations extend beyond financial assistance and encompass knowledge transfer, technical expertise, and capacity building efforts. Through coordinated endeavors, China has derived significant benefits from the global community's collective experience and resources.

In recent years, China has actively engaged with international organizations such as the World Bank, International Monetary Fund (IMF), United Nations Development Programme (UNDP), and various bilateral partners to reinforce its poverty reduction strategies. These collaborations have facilitated the implementation of innovative approaches and best practices in addressing poverty-related issues. Furthermore, international aid has contributed to the improvement of infrastructure, healthcare systems, and educational facilities in impoverished regions, bolstering the overall socio-economic development trajectory.

Additionally, foreign aid has supported China's endeavors in promoting sustainable livelihoods and environmental conservation. Many collaborative projects focus on empowering communities through skill development, entrepreneurship, and access to clean energy solutions, thereby fostering resilience and self-sufficiency. The exchange of knowledge and technological advancements has enabled the integration of sustainable practices into China's poverty alleviation framework, aligning with global efforts towards sustainable development goals.

Moreover, these collaborative efforts have emphasized the importance of inclusive growth and social welfare, aligning with China's commitment to leaving no one behind in its pursuit of eradicating poverty. Leveraging international aid and partnerships, China has not only expanded the reach and impact of its poverty reduction initiatives but also fostered greater understanding and cooperation across borders. The cross-cultural exchanges and mutual learning experiences have underlined the significance of solidarity and shared responsibility in addressing global challenges, including poverty alleviation.

Despite the notable benefits of international aid and collaborations, challenges persist in ensuring the efficient utilization of resources and the alignment of diverse stakeholders' objectives. Furthermore, effective coordination and monitoring mechanisms are essential to maximize the impact of international aid initiatives. Striking a balance between respecting national sovereignty and integrating external support harmoniously remains a critical consideration in fostering sustainable collaborations.

In conclusion, international aid and collaborations have emerged as powerful enablers in China's endeavor to combat poverty. The synergy between domestic efforts and global partnerships has amplified the transformative potential of poverty reduction programs, laying the groundwork for inclusive and sustainable development. Moving forward, fostering mutually beneficial collaborations and strengthening international solidarity will be integral to realizing the shared vision of a world free from poverty.

Challenges and Critiques of the Programs

Poverty reduction programs in China have faced various challenges and received critiques despite international aid and collaborations. One prominent challenge is the issue of targeting and reaching the most vulnerable populations. The vast size and diversity of China make it difficult to ensure that resources are effectively reaching those who need them most. Additionally, the criteria used to define poverty may not always accurately capture the complex realities faced by individuals and communities. As a result, there have been concerns about the inclusivity and accuracy of the poverty reduction programs.

Another challenge revolves around the sustainability of the initiatives. While significant progress has been made in lifting millions out of poverty, there are questions about the long-term impact and the ability to prevent relapses into poverty. This necessitates a shift from short-term interventions to comprehensive, sustainable measures that address not just income levels but also access to quality education, healthcare, and other essential services.

Furthermore, the effectiveness and transparency of governance mechanisms overseeing these poverty alleviation efforts have drawn scrutiny. Evident bureaucratic hurdles, corruption, and mismanagement can hamper the efficiency of aid distribution and program implementation, undermining the intended outcomes. In some cases, political motivations may influence resource allocation, leading to inequalities and inefficiencies within the system.

Critiques of the programs also touch upon the socio-economic implications. Some experts argue that while the focus has been on boosting incomes and consumption, attention must equally be directed towards systemic changes that empower marginalized populations and foster inclusive growth. There's a call for addressing underlying structural issues, such as land rights, social welfare, and labor rights, to create a more equitable society.

Additionally, there are debates surrounding the external influences on China's poverty reduction strategies. The increasing involvement of international organizations and donors raises questions about the degree of autonomy and the alignment of goals with China's national priorities. Balancing external support with domestic sovereignty and tailored approaches remains an intricate task.

It's crucial to recognize these challenges and critiques as opportunities for refinement and evolution. By acknowledging the complexities and potential shortcomings of existing poverty reduction programs, China can strive towards more impactful and sustainable solutions that leave no one behind.

DRIVERS OF ECONOMIC GROWTH

OVERVIEW OF ECONOMIC GROWTH FACTORS

Economic growth is the sustained increase in the real output of goods and services in an economy. It serves as a key indicator of the overall health and vitality of a country's economy, reflecting expanding opportunities for its citizens and businesses. Several crucial factors drive economic growth, each playing a distinctive role in shaping the trajectory of development within a nation. Firstly, technological advancements lay the groundwork for innovation and productivity gains, enabling industries to produce more with fewer resources. This, in turn, fosters economic expansion by increasing the overall efficiency and output of the economy. Additionally, investments in education and human capital contribute significantly to economic growth by enhancing the skills and knowledge base of the workforce, leading to higher levels of productivity and entrepreneurial activity. Furthermore, sound institutional frameworks, including property rights protection and the rule of law, create an environment conducive to stable, long-term economic growth by mitigating risks and establishing transparency in transactions. Moreover, the availability of capital, both physical and financial, fuels the expansion of businesses, allowing for the acquisition of new technologies and the development of infrastructure critical for growth. The interplay of these factors creates an environment ripe for economic expansion, acting as foundational components that set the stage for sustained prosperity and development.

Industrialization as a Catalyst for Growth

The process of industrialization has served as a catalyst for significant economic growth in numerous nations throughout history. By transitioning from agrarian-based economies to industrialized societies, countries have been able to leverage new technologies, increase productivity, and create diverse job opportunities. Industrialization fundamentally alters the structure of an economy, leading to enhanced efficiency and output. One pivotal aspect of industrialization is the development of manufacturing capabilities, which not only drives economic expansion but also spurs innovation and technological advancement. As industries evolve, they generate demand for skilled labor, thus fostering human capital development and a more educated workforce. This, in turn, contributes to sustained economic growth and facilitates the transition to a knowledge-based economy. Moreover, industrialization fosters urbanization as individuals migrate from rural areas to cities in search of employment opportunities provided by burgeoning industries. Urban centers become hubs of economic activity, attracting investment and further stimulating economic growth. The shift towards industrialization also brings about infrastructure development, including transportation networks and energy systems, laying the foundation for continued economic progress. Additionally, industrialization creates interconnected supply chains, promoting trade and specialization, thus allowing nations to capitalize on their comparative advantages. It is essential to recognize that while industrialization is associated with economic benefits, it also poses challenges such as environmental degradation and the need for sustainable resource management. Therefore, sustainable industrial practices must be integral to the framework of industrialization to ensure long-term prosperity. Overall, the impact of industrialization on economic growth is profound, reshaping societies, driving innovation, and propelling nations towards prosperity.

Urbanization Trends and Contributions to GDP

Urbanization plays a pivotal role in shaping a country's economic landscape, with profound implications for its Gross Domestic Product (GDP) and overall development. As rural populations migrate to urban areas, new opportunities arise, driving economic growth and transformation. In the context of China's economic trajectory, urbanization has been a critical driver of expansion, leading to a surge in productivity and innovation. The transition from agrarian-based economies to urban-centered societies has historically correlated with significant GDP growth, reflecting the impact of urbanization on industrial output, consumption patterns, and infrastructure investment. Moreover, urban centers serve as hubs of commerce, finance, and technological advancement, fostering an environment conducive to entrepreneurship and job creation. It is important to note that urbanization not only drives economic output but also contributes to social and cultural dynamism, facilitating the exchange of ideas, knowledge, and skills. The interconnectedness of urban areas within a national economy forms a network that enables the efficient allocation of resources, enhances market integration, and spurs specialization. Furthermore, the concentration of human capital in urban settings fuels innovation and facilitates the dissemination of best practices across industries, thus optimizing productivity and efficiency. However, it is essential to address the challenges associated with rapid urbanization, such as housing affordability, infrastructure strain, and environmental sustainability. Sustainable urban development strategies are crucial to mitigating these challenges and ensuring inclusive and equitable growth. By understanding the multifaceted impact of urbanization on GDP and socio-economic dynamics, policymakers can devise strategic interventions to harness the potential of urbanization while addressing its attendant complexities.

Technological Advancements and Competitiveness

Technological advancements have emerged as a cornerstone for fostering economic competitiveness in the contemporary global landscape. The integration of advanced technologies, such as artificial intelligence, big data analytics, and automation, has revolutionized traditional production processes, leading to enhanced productivity, efficiency, and innovation. Leveraging technological capabilities has become imperative for nations striving to maintain a competitive edge in the global economy. This section delves into the multifaceted relationship between technological advancements and economic competitiveness, scrutinizing the key dynamics and implications.

The adoption of cutting-edge technologies drives improvements in production processes and quality standards, paving the way for increased output and cost efficiencies. Furthermore, technological investments bolster the development of sophisticated infrastructure and digital ecosystems, crucial for propelling economic growth and attracting foreign direct investment. Advanced technological infrastructure also underpins the capacity for rapid information dissemination, thereby facilitating seamless global trade and integration into transnational value chains. As such, nations with robust technological frameworks are better positioned to optimize their industrial potential and assert competitiveness in the international market.

In addition to augmenting economic performance, embracing technological advancements contributes to fostering a knowledge-based economy. By investing in research and development initiatives, countries can catalyze the creation of high-value innovative products and services, fostering higher skilled employment opportunities and driving intellectual capital formation. Furthermore, technological prowess serves as an essential driver for enhancing human capital through specialized education and expertise in science, technology, engineering, and mathematics (STEM) disciplines. Consequently, a highly skilled and adaptable workforce becomes a pivotal factor in fortifying a nation's economic competitiveness on the global stage.

Moreover, the strategic alignment of technological advancements with sustainable practices engenders environmentally conscious production methodologies, reducing ecological footprints and empowering corporate social responsibility endeavors. Sustainable technological innovations offer pathways for achieving resource efficiency, environmental preservation, and mitigating climate impact, thus positioning nations favorably in an era of heightened environmental awareness and ethical consumerism. Harnessing technology to address sustainability challenges not only establishes ethical leadership but also opens avenues for new market segments and business diversification.

As nations navigate the complexities of the digital age, policy harmonization and regulatory frameworks play a decisive role in shaping the direction of technological progress and its impact on economic competitiveness. Governments need to foster an enabling environment through favorable policies that incentivize investment in R&D, cultivate digital skills, and promote inclusive access to technological resources. Furthermore, collaboration between public and private sectors is essential for steering national agendas towards techno-economic synergy and fostering an ecosystem conducive to continuous innovation and adaptability.

In conclusion, the symbiotic relationship between technological advancements and economic competitiveness underscores the paramount significance of integrating innovation and digitalization into national economic strategies. Embracing the transformative potential of technology can bolster a nation's capacity to navigate complex global markets, build resilient economies, and position itself as a formidable contender in the evolving landscape of international trade and commerce.

Government's Role in Economic Strategy

In the intricate web of economic growth, the role of government stands as a crucial determinant. Governments play a multifaceted role in shaping the economic destiny of their nations, from setting the strategic direction for sustainable growth to creating an enabling environment for businesses and industries. At the core of economic strategy lies the formulation and implementation of policies that facilitate growth while ensuring stability and equity. Governments serve as key stakeholders in orchestrating the various factors of production and influencing the overall economic landscape. Through targeted interventions and policy frameworks, they undertake the responsibility of steering the economy towards prosperity. A pivotal aspect of the government's role is the establishment of a conducive regulatory framework that fosters economic stability and mitigates risks. This involves creating transparent and consistent regulations, promoting fair competition, and safeguarding consumer interests. By providing clear guidelines and enforcing compliance, governments contribute to fostering a stable economic environment that encourages investment and entrepreneurial activities. Additionally, governments are entrusted with the task of aligning economic strategies with broader national objectives, such as social welfare, environmental sustainability, and global competitiveness. They do so by formulating policies that balance economic growth with social inclusiveness and environmental stewardship. Furthermore, the government plays a central role in allocating resources, enhancing infrastructure, and investing in human capital development, thereby laying the foundation for sustainable economic progress. Strategic planning and effective governance are imperative for leveraging resources efficiently and effectively, and the government is instrumental in driving these initiatives forward. Ultimately, the government's economic strategy encompasses not only short-term objectives but also long-term visions that encompass the nation's future trajectory. It requires a delicate balance between proactive policymaking, responsive regulation, and adaptability to dynamic global economic trends. As we delve deeper into the intricacies of economic strategy, it becomes evident that the government's role serves as a linchpin in shaping the economic fortunes of a nation, weaving together an overarching vision with actionable policies to propel sustainable growth.

Regulatory Frameworks Enhancing Economic Stability

Regulatory frameworks play a pivotal role in ensuring economic stability and fostering sustainable growth within a nation's economy. By establishing clear guidelines and standards for business practices, these regulations minimize the potential for market distortions, fraudulent activities, and excessive risk-taking that could jeopardize the overall financial system. Moreover, they contribute to creating an environment of trust and confidence among investors, businesses, and consumers, thereby promoting a healthy economic ecosystem.

One of the primary objectives of regulatory frameworks is to maintain fair and transparent market conditions. Through stringent oversight and enforcement, regulatory bodies can mitigate the adverse impacts of monopolistic behaviors, price manipulation, and insider trading, which might otherwise undermine the integrity of the market. By promoting healthy competition and preventing anticompetitive practices, these regulations safeguard the interests of both businesses and consumers, ultimately contributing to sustained economic equilibrium.

Furthermore, regulatory frameworks are instrumental in addressing systemic risks within the financial sector. By imposing prudential standards on banks, financial institutions, and capital markets, regulators aim to enhance the stability and resilience of the entire financial system. This includes requirements related to capital adequacy, risk management, and liquidity, which are crucial for mitigating the probability of financial crises and ensuring the continuity of essential financial services during times of economic turbulence.

In addition to mitigating risks, regulatory frameworks also facilitate the advancement of socially responsible business practices. By setting environmental, social, and governance (ESG) criteria, these regulations encourage businesses to operate in a manner that takes into account not only their financial performance but also their impact on society and the environment. This approach aligns with the broader goal of achieving sustainable development and promotes ethical business conduct, which is increasingly valued by conscientious consumers and investors alike.

Moreover, regulatory frameworks often serve as instruments for maintaining macroeconomic stability. By overseeing fiscal and monetary policies, regulatory authorities can influence variables such as inflation rates, interest rates, and exchange rates, thereby contributing to a more predictable and conducive economic environment. This predictability fosters investor confidence and facilitates long-term planning and investment decision-making, consequently stimulating economic growth.

While the importance of regulatory frameworks in enhancing economic stability cannot be overstated, it is imperative for these regulations to strike a delicate balance between promoting stability and fostering innovation and growth. Excessive or overly rigid regulations may inadvertently stifle entrepreneurship, hinder technological advancements, and impede market dynamism. Therefore, a nuanced and adaptive approach to regulation is necessary to accommodate the evolving nature of the economy and ensure that regulatory frameworks remain effective without unduly stifling innovation and progress.

Interlinkages between Industrialization, Urbanization, and Technology

Industrialization, urbanization, and technology are interconnected drivers that have played pivotal roles in propelling economic growth in various nations across the globe. The symbiotic relationship between these elements has been a defining feature of modern economic development, shaping the landscape of industries, cities, and innovation.

Industrialization serves as a cornerstone of economic advancement, fostering the transformation of agrarian societies into industrial powerhouses. The shift from manual labor to mechanized production revolutionizes productivity, leading to increased output and economic expansion. As industries thrive, urban centers emerge as hubs of opportunity, drawing in a swelling workforce seeking employment and livelihood. Urbanization, therefore, becomes an organic byproduct of industrial progress, with cities evolving into vibrant engines of commerce, culture, and community.

Simultaneously, technological advancements act as catalysts for both industrialization and urbanization, fueling their symbiotic relationship. Innovations in manufacturing processes, such as automation and precision engineering, not only optimize industrial output but also drive urban migration as workers seek to leverage their skills in technologically driven sectors. Furthermore, the digital revolution has birthed smart cities, where cutting-edge technologies underpin sustainable urban development, resource optimization, and enhanced quality of life.

The interplay of industrialization, urbanization, and technology is not confined within national borders; rather, it reverberates across global economies, shaping interconnected networks of trade, investment, and knowledge exchange. In this era of globalization, the triad of industrialization, urbanization, and technology serves as a linchpin in fostering international collaborations and competition. Cross-border supply chains fuel industrial growth, while urban centers magnetize diverse talents and ideas, becoming melting pots for cultural exchange and entrepreneurship.

Amidst these interlinkages, challenges and opportunities abound. Sustainable urban planning becomes imperative to mitigate environmental stresses arising from rapid industrial and urban expansion. Moreover, leveraging technology for inclusive growth and equitable access to opportunities emerges as a pressing concern.

Understanding the intricate dynamics of these interlinked forces is indispensable for policymakers, business leaders, and citizens alike as they navigate the evolving landscape of economic growth. By recognizing and harnessing the potential synergies between industrialization, urbanization, and technology, societies can chart a path towards sustainable prosperity and inclusive development.

Policy Measures for Sustainable Economic Growth

Sustainable economic growth is paramount for the long-term prosperity of any nation. To achieve and maintain sustainable growth, governments must implement a range of policy measures that address various aspects of the economy. One crucial policy area is investment in education and skill development. By ensuring a well-educated and skilled workforce, countries can enhance productivity and competitiveness, driving economic growth. Additionally, fostering innovation through supportive policies for research and development can lead to technological advancements and new industries, further stimulating economic expansion. Furthermore, creating a conducive environment for entrepreneurship and small business growth can spur job creation and diversify the economic landscape.

Another critical policy measure for sustainable economic growth is the adoption of responsible fiscal and monetary policies. By maintaining fiscal discipline, controlling government spending, and ensuring a balanced budget, countries can contribute to macroeconomic stability, which is essential for sustained growth. Moreover, implementing sound monetary policies, such as maintaining price stability and managing interest rates, can foster an environment of confidence and predictability, encouraging investment and capital formation. Equally important is the establishment of effective regulatory frameworks that promote fair competition, protect consumer rights, and ensure financial stability.

Sustainable economic growth also hinges on environmental sustainability. Governments need to integrate environmental considerations into their economic policies, striving for a balance between economic development and conservation of natural resources. Encouraging sustainable practices in industries, promoting renewable energy sources, and incentivizing eco-friendly initiatives are crucial steps towards sustainable economic growth. Additionally, promoting international trade while ensuring fair trade practices and participating in global efforts for economic cooperation and development can create opportunities for economic expansion while fostering global stability.

In conclusion, achieving sustainable economic growth requires a holistic approach to policy-making. Governments must prioritize investment in human capital, innovation, and entrepreneurship, while maintaining fiscal and monetary discipline and pursuing environmentally-responsible economic strategies. By leveraging these comprehensive policy measures, nations can lay the foundation for enduring and equitable economic growth that benefits current and future generations.

Case Studies: Successful Implementations of Economic Policies

In this section, we delve into the exploration of exemplary instances where economic policies have led to significant and sustainable growth in various countries. One noteworthy case study is that of South Korea, which, through a strategic approach under its 'Export-Oriented Industrialization' strategy, managed to transform from an agrarian economy to a high-tech industrial powerhouse within a short span. The government's deliberate focus on export-led growth, extensive infrastructure development, and investment in education and technology played pivotal roles in fostering rapid economic expansion.

Another compelling example is that of Singapore, where prudent economic planning and targeted policies propelled the nation from a developing state to a global financial hub. By embracing an open economy model, prioritizing investments in human capital, and establishing an efficient taxation system, Singapore effectively attracted foreign direct investments and multinational corporations, paving the way for unparalleled economic success.

Moreover, the economic reforms undertaken by India in the early 1990s serve as a remarkable illustration of policy-driven transformation. Through liberalization, privatization, and globalization initiatives, India experienced substantial growth in sectors such as information technology, telecommunications, and manufacturing, propelling the country onto the global economic stage.

On the African continent, Botswana stands out as a distinctive case study, having implemented prudent economic policies combined with effective governance. With careful management of its diamond resources and investments in education and healthcare, Botswana achieved remarkable progress, surpassing many other African nations in terms of economic development and social indicators.

Additionally, the case of Germany post-World War II showcases strategic policy implementations that spurred an impressive economic revival. Focusing on rebuilding infrastructure, promoting innovation, and investing in vocational training, Germany rapidly transformed into a leading industrial power.

These case studies underscore the significance of tailored economic policies and strategic interventions in driving sustainable growth and socioeconomic development. By analyzing these examples, valuable insights can be gleaned for formulating well-informed economic strategies that are attuned to diverse national contexts and conducive to fostering long-term prosperity and progress.

Future Outlook and Challenges

As we look towards the future, it is essential to anticipate the challenges that may impede sustainable economic growth while also acknowledging the potential opportunities that lie ahead. One of the foremost challenges arises from the rapid pace of technological innovation, which can both drive growth and disrupt traditional economic structures. Embracing these advancements while mitigating their potential negative effects will be vital. Additionally, the increasing interconnectedness of global markets brings about heightened vulnerability to external shocks and economic downturns. Mitigating these risks through effective risk management practices and international cooperation will be imperative for safeguarding economic stability. Another significant facet of the future outlook pertains to environmental sustainability. As economies expand, the strain on natural resources intensifies, necessitating a shift towards cleaner and more sustainable practices. Failure to address this challenge could lead to irreversible ecological damage with profound implications for future generations. In the realm of geopolitics, evolving geopolitical dynamics pose both opportunities and risks. The shifting power structures and geopolitical tensions could potentially disrupt global economic interdependencies, highlighting the need for strategic diplomacy and conflict resolution. Moreover, an aging population in many developed economies presents a formidable demographic challenge, with potential implications for labor force participation and social welfare systems. Addressing this demographic shift will call for innovative solutions and policy reforms. Amidst these challenges, however, lie promising opportunities. The continued expansion of digital technologies offers avenues for enhanced productivity and efficiency gains. Furthermore, the rising middle-class populations in various emerging economies present new markets and consumer bases, fostering prospects for increased trade and investment. An emphasis on fostering inclusive growth that benefits all segments of society is critical for sustained development. Successfully navigating these complexities requires visionary leadership, robust governance structures, and proactive policy responses. By addressing these challenges head-on and capitalizing on the associated opportunities, nations can steer towards a future of balanced, sustainable, and inclusive economic growth.

CHINA'S STATE-CAPITALIST MODEL

OVERVIEW OF CHINA'S ECONOMIC SYSTEM

China's economic system is often characterized as a unique blend of market-oriented strategies and state intervention. This mixed economy incorporates elements of capitalism, socialism, and state control to create what is commonly referred to as the 'Chinese Model.' One of the key distinguishing features of this economic system is the significant presence of state-owned enterprises (SOEs) across various sectors. These SOEs, often representing strategic industries such as energy, telecommunications, and finance, play a pivotal role in driving the country's economic agenda. State ownership allows the government to influence production, investment, and resource allocation, ensuring alignment with national objectives and priorities. In addition, the Chinese government exercises considerable control over key facets of the economy through concerted regulation and planning. This includes interventions in currency exchange rates, industrial policies, and strategic development initiatives aimed at bolstering domestic industries. Moreover, the Chinese economic system actively encourages private enterprise and foreign investment while maintaining tight regulatory oversight. This approach has led to the rapid growth of a dynamic private sector that co-exists alongside state-owned entities, contributing significantly to the overall economic landscape. Another noteworthy aspect of China's economic framework is its embrace of technological innovation and digital transformation. The government has integrated these priorities into its economic strategy, culminating in substantial investments in research and development, technology infrastructure, and the adoption of advanced technologies such as artificial intelligence and big data analytics. Furthermore, the interconnectedness between the state, businesses, and financial institutions underscores the synergistic relationship between the public and private spheres to advance economic prosperity. Overall, understanding the intricacies of China's economic system necessitates an appreciation of its hybrid nature, where market forces interact with deliberate state guidance and regulation, shaping a distinct model that has garnered global attention and scrutiny.

Defining State Capitalism

In understanding the concept of state capitalism, it is imperative to delve into its intricate and multifaceted dimensions. State capitalism is an economic system in which the state plays a significant role in the operation and management of the economy, often through state-owned enterprises (SOEs) and government intervention in various economic activities. Unlike traditional capitalist systems characterized by free-market mechanisms and minimal state interference, state capitalism entails direct state involvement in economic decision-making, resource allocation, and industrial planning. This approach allows the government to exert influence over strategic industries, key sectors, and national development priorities. As such, state capitalism reflects a departure from conventional laissez-faire capitalism and introduces a model where the state assumes a proactive role in shaping economic outcomes. One distinguishing feature of state capitalism is the heightened integration of political and economic objectives, as the state leverages its authority to pursue both social and commercial aims in a coordinated manner. Furthermore, state capitalism can manifest in diverse forms, with variations in the degree of state ownership, market regulation, and the balance between public and private sector participation. This heterogeneity ensures that state capitalism is adaptable to different national contexts and developmental strategies. It is vital to recognize that the dynamics of state capitalism are influenced by historical, political, and cultural factors specific to each country, contributing to nuanced variations in its application and impact. The concept of state capitalism has garnered increased attention in contemporary discourse, particularly in the context of China's rapid economic ascendancy and its distinct model of integrating state direction with market forces. By examining the principles, characteristics, and implications of state capitalism, one gains insight into the shifting landscape of global economics and the varying approaches adopted by nations in fostering economic development.

Components of the State-Capitalist System

The state-capitalist system in China is characterized by a unique combination of state control and a market-oriented economy. Its components encompass various areas that shape the country's economic landscape. One key component is the presence of state-owned enterprises (SOEs), which play a significant role in strategic industries such as energy, telecommunications, and finance. These SOEs are crucial to the government's ability to influence and steer the direction of the economy through direct intervention and control. Additionally, the state exerts influence through its ownership of land and urban real estate, thereby being able to guide urbanization and infrastructure development in line with its economic objectives. Another component is the state's involvement in financial institutions; this allows the government to dictate credit allocation, interest rates, and overall monetary policy, ultimately influencing the flow of capital within the economy. Furthermore, the state-capitalist system features a distinct approach to industrial policy, with the government implementing targeted plans to foster certain industries, technologies, and innovation. This proactive industrial policy is instrumental in propelling strategic sectors forward and achieving technological advancements at a national level. The government also plays a pivotal role in shaping the direction of research and development, working in tandem with private enterprises and academic institutions to drive innovation and technological progress. Moreover, the system encompasses a dynamic regulatory framework where the government exercises authority over markets, trade, and foreign investment, reflecting a deliberate effort to safeguard national interests in the global arena. An additional facet is the role of the state in public welfare and social security, ensuring social stability alongside economic development. These components collectively formulate a complex, interwoven system where the state exercises substantial influence over the economic landscape, steering it towards predetermined goals and priorities.

Role of Government in Economic Planning

In China's state-capitalist model, the government plays a pivotal role in economic planning, setting long-term development goals and formulating policies to achieve them. The government exercises a high degree of influence over strategic industries and key sectors, leveraging its power to steer the direction of economic growth. Through five-year plans and other policy instruments, the government allocates resources, subsidizes targeted industries, and directs investment towards priority areas such as infrastructure, technology, and social welfare programs. This proactive approach enables the government to shape the trajectory of the economy towards sustainable and inclusive development. Centralized decision-making allows for quick implementation of economic reforms and initiatives, ensuring that the overall national development agenda is effectively pursued. Moreover, the government's involvement extends to fostering innovation and entrepreneurship through financial support, research grants, and regulatory frameworks that encourage risk-taking and experimentation. By guiding the allocation of capital and resources, the government actively manages industrial restructuring, promotes technological advancement, and cultivates new growth engines, thereby shaping the competitive landscape and positioning the nation for global leadership in key sectors. The government's interventions are underpinned by a complex web of incentives, regulations, and performance targets designed to align private-sector activities with broader developmental priorities. Moreover, the government's emphasis on public-private partnerships and collaboration creates an environment where businesses are encouraged to contribute to national objectives while benefiting from the state's strategic guidance and support. This coordinated approach reflects a deep intertwining of political and economic imperatives, emphasizing the symbiotic relationship between the state and the market. However, this level of government intervention also raises important considerations regarding market efficiency, resource allocation, and regulatory transparency, which will be explored in subsequent sections of this book.

GDP Growth Analysis

China's GDP growth has been a focal point of international attention in recent decades, reflecting the nation's remarkable economic transformation. The sustained and rapid expansion of China's economy has significantly contributed to global economic dynamics. Examining the underlying drivers of this growth reveals a multifaceted evolution rooted in institutional reforms, globalization, and innovative policy initiatives. Key contributors to the impressive GDP growth have included robust domestic consumption, surging export performance, and substantial investments in infrastructure and technology. Furthermore, China's proactive approach to economic planning, including strategic resource allocation and development programs, has underscored its commitment to achieving sustained, high-quality growth. This has generated opportunities for increased productivity, employment, and income levels across various sectors, thereby supporting the nation's socio-economic stability and broader global economic integration. It is essential to assess the qualitative aspects of GDP growth, such as environmental sustainability, income distribution, and social welfare, in order to comprehensively evaluate the significance and impacts of China's economic progress. As China continues its journey towards a more sustainable and balanced economic model, the analysis of GDP growth provides valuable insights into the nation's evolving role in shaping the global economic landscape.

Infrastructure Development Advances

China's state-capitalist model has facilitated monumental leaps in infrastructure development, positioning the country as a global leader in this domain. The scale and speed of China's infrastructure expansion are unparalleled in modern history. The strategic vision and meticulous planning by the government have resulted in the construction of extensive networks of highways, railways, airports, and seaports across the nation. State-owned enterprises, with substantial government support, have been instrumental in executing these ambitious projects. The high-speed rail network, for instance, stands as a testament to China's prowess in infrastructure development. Spanning tens of thousands of kilometers, this network has significantly reduced travel times and opened up new economic opportunities for both urban and rural areas. Furthermore, China's futuristic megaprojects, such as the Beijing Daxing International Airport and the Hong Kong-Zhuhai-Macau Bridge, showcase the country's commitment to pushing the boundaries of innovation and engineering. The construction of smart cities equipped with advanced technologies exemplifies China's holistic approach to urban development, integrating infrastructure with environmental sustainability and digital connectivity. Notably, the Belt and Road Initiative (BRI) demonstrates China's proactive stance in fostering international infrastructure interconnectivity. By investing in critical infrastructure projects in various countries, China aims to enhance global trade and create mutual economic benefits. The transformative impact of China's infrastructure endeavors is not limited to domestic enrichment; it extends to influencing international dynamics, reshaping global trade routes, and fostering diplomatic ties. While China's infrastructure achievements are undeniable, they also raise questions about environmental impact, debt sustainability, and geopolitical implications. As we delve deeper into China's state-capitalist model, understanding the interplay between infrastructure development and these multifaceted concerns becomes imperative.

Technological Innovation under State Guidance

Technological innovation in China has been significantly influenced by the government's guidance and support. The state-capitalist system has played a central role in fostering technological advancements through strategic initiatives and investments. Under the guidance of the government, China has experienced remarkable progress in various technological domains, including but not limited to, telecommunications, artificial intelligence, renewable energy, and advanced manufacturing.

The government's active involvement in fostering technological innovation is manifested through initiatives such as the 'Made in China 2025' plan, which aims to transform China into a high-tech powerhouse by prioritizing sectors such as robotics, aerospace, and new energy vehicles. Moreover, the implementation of national strategies like the 'Internet Plus' initiative has further propelled the integration of internet technologies with traditional industries, thereby driving innovation and efficiency.

Furthermore, the state's substantial investments in research and development have spurred scientific breakthroughs and technological advancements. The establishment of various state-supported research centers, technology parks, and incubators has provided crucial resources and incentives for scientists, innovators, and entrepreneurs to drive forward groundbreaking projects.

It is important to note that while state guidance has been instrumental in propelling China's technological prowess, it has also raised concerns regarding intellectual property rights, market competition, and ethical considerations. The government's intervention in promoting domestic champions and protecting key industries has prompted scrutiny from international stake-holders.

Despite these challenges, China's state-guided approach to technological innovation has undeniably contributed to its transformation into a global leader in several technological fields. This chapter will illuminate the intricacies of this phenomenon and explore its implications for China's economic landscape, international relations, and the broader global technological ecosystem.

Integration with Global Markets

China's integration with global markets has redefined the dynamics of international trade and investment. Leveraging its state-capitalist model, China has effectively tapped into global markets by showcasing its competitive advantages in various sectors. The country's proactive approach towards trade liberalization and participation in international organizations, such as the World Trade Organization (WTO), has facilitated closer economic ties with other nations. Furthermore, the Belt and Road Initiative (BRI) serves as a pivotal mechanism for extending China's influence across continents, fostering infrastructure development, and promoting interconnectedness among participating countries. This ambitious initiative aims to enhance trade routes and connectivity, thereby fortifying China's role in the global economy. At the same time, China's establishment of free trade zones and preferential trade agreements has propelled its collaboration with diverse economies, creating a favorable environment for cross-border investments and commerce. The nation's focus on technology, innovation, and high-quality manufacturing has allowed it to position itself as a key player in global value chains, shaping the landscape of international commerce and bolstering its export capabilities. Moreover, China's active engagement in global financial institutions has further solidified its position in the international monetary system, enabling the yuan's inclusion in the International Monetary Fund's Special Drawing Rights basket. Embracing globalization, China has prioritized multilateral cooperation, advocating for open markets, sustainable development, and fair trade practices. However, the increasing interconnectedness has also exposed China to complex challenges related to market access, intellectual property rights, and geopolitical tensions with traditional economic powers. As China continues to navigate its integration with global markets, the evolving dynamics of international trade and the implications of economic interdependence remain crucial factors that shape the trajectory of both China's state-capitalist model and the global economy at large.

Comparison with Other Economic Models

In comparing China's state-capitalist model with other economic systems such as the free-market model prevalent in Western countries, it is essential to assess various aspects that distinguish these approaches. One of the key differentiators is the level of government intervention and control in shaping the economy. In contrast to the laissez-faire approach seen in free-market economies, China's state-capitalist model actively involves government direction and regulation. This stark contrast influences policies related to industrial planning, resource allocation, and market interventions.

Moreover, the role of state-owned enterprises (SOEs) sets the Chinese model apart from others. While free-market economies rely predominantly on private entities to drive economic growth, China's model is characterized by a significant presence of SOEs across strategic sectors. This influence extends beyond domestic activities, with SOEs often playing a crucial role in international markets, thereby illustrating the unique blend of state and capital in China's economic landscape.

Furthermore, the emphasis on long-term planning and stability in China's economic vision stands in marked divergence from the more short-term-oriented strategies prevalent in the West. This contrasts not only in terms of policy formulation but also affects investment patterns and risk assessments. China's state capitalism draws from a legacy of central planning and collective leadership which shapes the decision-making processes and priorities, while free-market economies are driven more by individual enterprise and competitive forces.

Additionally, the response mechanisms to economic challenges differ significantly between these models. While the decentralized nature of free-market economies often allows for quicker adjustments in response to market fluctuations, China's state-capitalist system may adopt a more deliberate and coordinated approach, leveraging its comprehensive economic blueprint to maneuver through both internal and external disruptions.

This comparison illustrates the diverse paths adopted by different economic models and prompts an exploration of the inherent strengths and weaknesses within each system. As global dynamics continue to evolve, discerning the implications and outcomes of these divergent models becomes increasingly critical for policymakers, businesses, and individuals navigating the complex interplay of global economies.

Summary and Transition to Challenges

In summarizing China's state-capitalist model and comparing it with other economic systems, it becomes evident that despite its tremendous achievements, the Chinese economic model faces unique challenges. The transition from a centrally planned economy to a more market-oriented system has driven exceptional growth, with impressive strides in infrastructure development, rapid technological innovation under state guidance, and remarkable integration with global markets. However, as China continues to mature economically and play a more significant role on the international stage, it confronts critical challenges associated with sustaining its growth momentum.

One of the foremost challenges lies in ensuring that the centralized decision-making does not stifle entrepreneurial creativity and innovation. Balancing state intervention and free market forces without impeding the dynamism of private enterprises calls for comprehensive and delicate policy adjustments. Moreover, the issue of income inequality and regional disparities emerges as a crucial concern. While coastal regions have enjoyed significant advancements, rural and inland areas continue to lag behind, posing complexities in achieving balanced and inclusive growth.

Furthermore, as China navigates towards a knowledge-based economy, the quality and sustainability of its economic growth come into focus. Environmental degradation, over-dependence on manufacturing, and the need for transitioning to higher value-added industries constitute formidable challenges. A closer examination also brings to light the vital necessity of addressing corporate governance and financial transparency issues to bolster investor confidence and foster a robust, resilient financial sector.

Amid these challenges, the shifting dynamics of international trade relations present additional complexities for the Chinese state-capitalist model. Geopolitical tensions, protectionist measures, and global economic uncertainties necessitate adept maneuvering to ensure continued access to vital markets while driving technological and industrial upgrading for sustainable competitive advantage. Additionally, demographic shifts and an aging population amplify the urgency of reforming social welfare systems and pension structures to counterbalance potential labor force constraints and achieve social stability.

As the global landscape evolves, China must proactively adapt to meet the demands of the future economy while confronting both domestic and international challenges. The ensuing chapters will delve deeper into these multifaceted issues, offering insights into the imperative strategies required for navigating through transformative phases and ensuring the continued success of the state-capitalist model within the broader context of the global economy.

CHALLENGES WITHIN CHINA'S MODEL

OVERVIEW OF CHINA'S CURRENT ECONOMIC MODEL

China's current economic model is a unique combination of state intervention and capitalist principles, often referred to as a state-capitalist approach. This model has played a pivotal role in driving the country's remarkable economic growth over the past few decades. At its core, China's state-capitalist approach involves a strong state presence in key sectors of the economy, strategic state-led investments, and the utilization of market mechanisms to drive growth. This hybrid framework has allowed China to achieve high levels of industrialization and economic expansion while maintaining strong government control. One of the fundamental implications of this model is the ability of the government to steer economic development in desired directions, such as prioritizing certain industries or regions for growth. This level of central planning has enabled China to rapidly modernize its infrastructure and boost productivity in key sectors. However, it also raises concerns about potential inefficiencies and misallocation of resources. The intertwining of state and market dynamics in China's economic model has also led to complex relationships between the public and private sectors. State-owned enterprises (SOEs) continue to hold significant influence and dominance in strategic industries, impacting competition and innovation. Additionally, China's state-capitalist approach has allowed the government to leverage its control over financial institutions to direct investment flows, mitigate risks, and maintain stability in times of economic flux. Nevertheless, critics argue that this has also resulted in the accumulation of debt and nonperforming assets, posing systemic risks to the overall economy. Overall, China's state-capitalist model presents a dynamic interplay between state power and market forces, offering a unique lens through which to examine the complexities of contemporary economic paradigms and the challenges inherent in balancing centralized governance with free-market principles.

Environmental Challenges in a Rapidly Industrializing Economy

Industrialization has been a major catalyst for China's economic growth, but it has also posed significant environmental challenges. As the nation rapidly industrialized, it witnessed unprecedented levels of air and water pollution, alongside ecological degradation. The heavy reliance on coal-powered plants and the rapid expansion of manufacturing industries contributed to severe air pollution, leading to public health concerns and environmental damage. Furthermore, irresponsible disposal of industrial waste resulted in widespread water contamination, making potable water sources increasingly scarce. The environmental challenges arising from rapid industrialization have drawn attention not just within China, but also internationally. Addressing these challenges demands comprehensive policies and practices that prioritize sustainable development and environmental preservation. China has initiated ambitious measures to combat environmental degradation, such as transitioning towards renewable energy sources, implementing stringent emission standards, and investing in green technologies. The government has also launched large-scale afforestation projects and enforced stricter regulations on industrial waste management. In addition to domestic efforts, international collaboration and knowledge exchange have played significant roles in addressing these challenges. Through partnerships with other nations and active participation in global environmental initiatives, China is demonstrating its commitment to mitigating the adverse environmental impact of its rapid industrialization. Despite these efforts, there remain complexities and trade-offs inherent in balancing economic growth with environmental sustainability. The transition to a more sustainable and environmentally conscious economy requires navigating intricate policy decisions, technological innovations, and sociopolitical considerations. Moreover, addressing environmental challenges in a rapidly industrializing economy involves fostering public awareness and participation in environmental conservation efforts. The enduring success of China's battle against environmental challenges rests on evolving policies, persistent enforcement, technological innovation, and societal engagement. As China continues to navigate the intersection of rapid industrialization and environmental sustainability, the outcomes will undoubtedly resonate globally and shape the future trajectory of our planet's ecosystem.

Addressing Air and Water Pollution: Policies and Practices

China's rapid industrialization has brought about an unprecedented level of air and water pollution, posing significant challenges to public health and environmental sustainability. The government has recognized the urgency of addressing this issue and has implemented a series of ambitious policies and practices to mitigate pollution levels. One such initiative is the Air Pollution Prevention and Control Action Plan, which targets a reduction in fine particulate matter (PM2.5) concentration, a major contributor to respiratory diseases. This plan includes measures such as the promotion of clean energy, stricter emission standards for industries, and the development of comprehensive air quality monitoring systems. Additionally, China has been actively promoting the use of renewable energy sources such as solar and wind power to reduce reliance on coal and other fossil fuels. Water pollution is also a pressing concern, and the government has established the Water Ten Plan to improve water quality across the country. This plan comprises stringent regulations on industrial wastewater discharge, the preservation of water resources, and the treatment of polluted bodies of water. Moreover, the implementation of ecological conservation projects has been instrumental in protecting vital water sources and restoring damaged ecosystems. Collaboration with international organizations and adoption of advanced technologies have been pivotal in enhancing China's capacity to address pollution challenges. Numerous public-private partnerships have emerged to drive innovation in pollution control, waste management, and sustainable urban development. While China has made considerable strides in combating pollution, the road ahead is demanding. Continued efforts are required to ensure the effective enforcement of environmental regulations and the integration of eco-friendly practices in industrial and agricultural sectors. Furthermore, raising public awareness and fostering a culture of environmental responsibility are crucial for the long-term success of these initiatives. By leveraging technological advancements, bolstering regulatory frameworks, and fostering cooperation at home and abroad, China is poised to overcome the daunting challenge of air and water pollution while paving the way for a cleaner, more sustainable future.

Economic Inequality: Regional Disparities and Income Gaps

Economic inequality within China has been a persistent issue, characterized by significant regional disparities and income gaps that have drawn attention both domestically and internationally. At the heart of this problem lies the imbalanced distribution of economic growth and development across various regions in the country. Urban areas, particularly along the eastern coast, have experienced rapid economic expansion and wealth accumulation, leading to stark disparities when compared to rural and inland regions. This divide has exacerbated issues such as limited access to quality education, healthcare, and employment opportunities in less developed areas, perpetuating a cycle of inequality. Furthermore, income gaps between different demographic groups have widened, with rural populations and migrant workers often finding themselves at a disadvantage compared to their urban counterparts. The government has recognized these challenges and acknowledged the need for targeted policies to address the root causes. Initiatives aimed at poverty alleviation, rural revitalization, and regional development have been introduced to bridge the gap between affluent and impoverished areas. These efforts have included investment in infrastructure, education, and social welfare programs to uplift underprivileged communities. However, despite these measures, achieving equitable distribution of wealth and resources remains an ongoing struggle. The complexities of addressing economic inequality are compounded by the interconnected nature of factors influencing disparities, including industrial growth patterns, land rights, and migration trends. As China continues on its path of economic transformation and global integration, it becomes increasingly imperative to find sustainable solutions that promote inclusive growth and reduce regional disparities. The willingness to confront these challenges head-on reflects not only a commitment to social justice but also a recognition of the broader benefits that an equitable and harmonious society can bring to the nation as a whole.

Efforts to Reduce Inequality: Government Initiatives and Outcomes

In response to the persistent challenge of economic inequality and regional disparities, the Chinese government has implemented a series of initiatives aimed at reducing these disparities and promoting inclusive growth. One of the pivotal efforts has been the targeted poverty alleviation campaign, which aims to lift millions of people out of poverty by focusing on specific regions and populations that are most in need. Through this initiative, the government has invested significant resources in infrastructure development, education, healthcare, and social welfare programs in impoverished areas, thereby addressing the root causes of economic inequality.

Moreover, the government has also pursued policies to promote urban-rural integration, recognizing the stark divide between rural and urban communities. This has involved initiatives such as the reform of the hukou (household registration) system, aimed at providing rural migrants with access to urban services and opportunities. By facilitating the movement of labor and capital across regions, these efforts seek to bridge the gap between rural and urban incomes, fostering more equitable economic development across the country.

The outcomes of these initiatives have been notable, with millions of people lifted out of poverty and a significant reduction in regional income gaps. The government's focus on targeted poverty alleviation has resulted in improved living standards, increased access to education and healthcare, and enhanced social mobility for those previously marginalized. Furthermore, the urban-rural integration policies have led to greater equality in employment opportunities and improved livelihoods for rural migrant workers, contributing to a more balanced and harmonious society.

While progress has been made, challenges remain in sustaining these efforts and ensuring that the benefits of economic development are equitably distributed. There is an ongoing need for continued investment in rural infrastructure, healthcare, and education, as well as the implementation of effective social safety nets to prevent individuals from falling back into poverty. Additionally, addressing the disparities between different regions and sectors of the economy requires a comprehensive and coordinated approach, taking into account the unique circumstances of each locality and demographic group.

Looking ahead, the government is committed to advancing its efforts to reduce inequality and foster shared prosperity. This includes a focus on promoting innovation and entrepreneurship in underdeveloped regions, fostering a more inclusive financial system, and further expanding access to essential social services. By continuing to prioritize inclusive growth and addressing the multifaceted nature of economic inequality, China aims to build a more equitable and sustainable economic future for all its citizens.

Human Rights Concerns: Freedom and Labor Conditions

The issue of human rights in China, particularly in relation to freedom and labor conditions, stands as a critical concern within the global discourse. In examining freedom, it is imperative to acknowledge the limitations imposed on freedom of expression and association, as well as the restrictions imposed on individuals and organizations that act against the state's interests. These restrictions are evident in the curtailment of press freedoms, censorship of online content, and prosecution of dissidents, highlighting the delicate balance between societal harmony and individual liberties.

Moreover, when assessing labor conditions, the focus shifts to the working environment, workers' rights, and the prevalence of labor exploitation. In pursuit of economic growth and development, China's industrial powerhouse has created millions of job opportunities, but concurrently exposed numerous workers to unsafe workplaces, inadequate compensation, and excessive work hours. These challenges have led to debates surrounding the need for enhanced labor protection laws and enforcement mechanisms to safeguard worker rights and promote fair labor practices.

While these concerns persist, it is essential to recognize the Chinese government's efforts to address human rights issues and improve labor conditions. Reforms aimed at strengthening labor laws, enhancing workplace safety standards, and combatting discrimination have been initiated, reflecting a willingness to mitigate such challenges. Additionally, the introduction of measures to promote collective bargaining and provide social security benefits demonstrates a commitment to enhancing the welfare of the labor force.

However, the implementation and effectiveness of these reforms remain subjects of scrutiny and debate. The intricacies of governance, economic priorities, and institutional barriers present formidable obstacles in realizing substantial progress in upholding human rights and improving labor conditions. The perpetual evolution of China's socio-economic landscape further complicates the resolution of these issues, demanding comprehensive approaches that integrate diverse perspectives from stakeholders.

Amidst these complexities, the intersection of human rights, freedom, and labor conditions in China embodies a multifaceted dilemma that necessitates nuanced strategies. As the nation continues to navigate its socio-political and economic trajectory, striking a harmonious equilibrium between fostering economic prosperity and safeguarding fundamental human rights emerges as an imperative mission. By critically evaluating these interconnected issues, stakeholders can cultivate an inclusive dialogue and formulate sustainable pathways towards creating a more equitable society.

Balancing Economic Growth with Human Rights: Strategies and Dilemmas

As China strives to maintain its economic growth while grappling with human rights concerns, the inherent complexities and challenges become increasingly apparent. The strategies employed by the Chinese government in achieving this delicate balance require a multifaceted approach that acknowledges the interdependence of economic prosperity and human rights. One of the key dilemmas lies in harmonizing the imperatives of economic progress with the fundamental tenets of human rights and individual freedoms. The government has pursued an array of policies aimed at addressing this complex issue, but tensions persist. The sustained push for economic development often intersects with the necessity of labor force mobilization, prompting debates about the protection of workers' rights and the preservation of personal liberties. Moreover, the quest for industrial and technological advancement needs to be reconciled with the environmental implications and the rights of affected communities. Efforts to mitigate these challenges are underway, but the ultimate equilibrium between economic growth and human rights preservation remains elusive. Among the strategies being implemented is a comprehensive legal framework that seeks to safeguard fundamental human rights while fostering a conducive environment for economic expansion. The adoption of labor laws and regulations, socio-economic reforms, and initiatives to curb discrimination in the workplace reflect the government's recognition of the need to address these critical issues. Furthermore, endeavors towards greater transparency and accountability are being undertaken to ensure that economic progress does not come at the expense of civil liberties. However, despite these efforts, divergences persist, compelling policymakers to confront the inherent dilemmas head-on. Effectively balancing economic priorities with human rights imperatives also necessitates international engagement and cross-border cooperation. China's participation in global dialogues on human rights issues underscores its willingness to collaborate with the international community in seeking viable solutions. Concurrently, the pursuit of sustainable development and green technologies emerges as a pivotal aspect of reconciling economic growth with human rights. By embracing environmentally friendly practices and investing in clean energy initiatives, China aims to demonstrate its commitment to both economic vitality and ecological preservation. Nevertheless, navigating the complexities of this dual commitment presents ongoing challenges and demands continual adaptability. As China charts its course towards comprehensive and sustainable development, the pursuit of an optimal equilibrium between economic growth and human rights upholds its status as a critical global concern, reflective of the intricate interplay between prosperity and human dignity.

Sustainable Development and Green Technologies

In the pursuit of sustainable development, China has recognized the critical importance of embracing green technologies across various sectors of its economy. The country has faced increasing pressure to mitigate its environmental impact while sustaining rapid economic growth. As a result, China has committed substantial resources to develop and implement green technologies aimed at reducing carbon emissions, conserving natural resources, and fostering eco-friendly practices. One of the key focal points has been the promotion of renewable energy sources, such as wind, solar, and hydropower. China has emerged as a global leader in renewable energy investment and capacity, with ambitious targets for further expansion. Through initiatives like the Belt and Road Initiative, China has also sought to export its green technologies to other nations, thereby promoting sustainability on a global scale. Additionally, the integration of green technologies into urban planning and infrastructure development has been pivotal in addressing environmental challenges. From the construction of eco-friendly buildings to the implementation of efficient public transportation systems, China has demonstrated a commitment to building sustainable cities. Moreover, the adoption of innovative technologies for waste management, pollution control, and ecological conservation has played a pivotal role in minimizing environmental degradation. Despite these efforts, challenges persist in fully realizing the potential of green technologies. Obstacles such as technological barriers, financial constraints, and regulatory complexities pose significant hurdles.

Furthermore, the need to balance economic imperatives with environmental stewardship remains an ongoing dilemma. Critically evaluating the trade-offs between short-term economic gains and long-term ecological sustainability is essential in charting a harmonious path forward. China's endeavor to embrace sustainable development and green technologies reflects a profound shift towards prioritizing environmental preservation alongside economic prosperity. By proactively addressing these challenges, China aims to cultivate a model of growth that is not only economically robust but also environmentally responsible, inspiring global action towards a more sustainable future.

International Criticism and Domestic Responses

Amid China's rapid economic ascent, international criticism has increasingly focused on various aspects of its economic model. One substantial area of contention centers on environmental sustainability and the impact of China's industrialization on global climate change. Environmental advocates and policymakers across the world have expressed concerns about China's high levels of greenhouse gas emissions, air pollution, and water contamination. This has prompted calls for greater accountability and transparency in China's environmental policies, as well as international cooperation to address these urgent challenges.

On the domestic front, Chinese authorities have recognized the imperative to counteract mounting environmental and social pressures. In response to international criticism, the Chinese government has implemented a series of initiatives aimed at addressing environmental issues, including ambitious targets for reducing carbon emissions and transitioning towards renewable energy sources. Moreover, China has initiated significant investments into green technologies, such as solar and wind power, signaling a commitment to enhancing environmental sustainability domestically and exerting positive influence on the global stage.

Aside from environmental concerns, international scrutiny of China's economic model extends to human rights and labor conditions. Critics have pointed out issues related to freedom of speech, press, and assembly, as well as labor rights and working conditions. Such criticisms have prompted a reassessment of China's policies both within the country and abroad. Domestically, government efforts have been made to improve labor standards and working conditions, with initiatives focusing on strengthening worker protection laws and promoting workplace safety measures. Furthermore, steps have been taken to gradually enhance civil liberties, albeit within parameters set by the government.

The interplay between international criticism and domestic responses underscores the evolving nature of China's economic transformation. It reflects a dynamic interrelationship between internal policy adjustments and external pressures exerted by global stakeholders. As China continues to navigate the complexities of international economic integration, the duality of embracing sustainable growth while addressing criticism will undoubtedly shape its future trajectory and global standing.

Future Prospects: Sustainability within China's Growth Paradigm

As China continues to grapple with sustainability challenges within its economic model, the future prospects of achieving a harmonious balance between growth and environmental preservation are pivotal. The shift towards sustainability within China's growth paradigm requires multifaceted strategies and concerted efforts across various sectors and stakeholders. One key aspect that underlines the future prospects is the alignment of economic development with environmental conservation. This entails integrating sustainable practices in industrial production, transitioning to cleaner energy sources, and implementing rigorous pollution control measures. Additionally, fostering innovation and investment in green technologies can bolster the prospects of a sustainable growth paradigm. The proliferation of eco-friendly initiatives, such as renewable energy projects and sustainable infrastructure development, is instrumental in steering China towards a more sustainable trajectory. Furthermore, it is imperative to address the social dimension of sustainability by focusing on improving the quality of life for citizens while mitigating the environmental impact. This involves promoting equitable access to resources, enhancing social welfare systems, and prioritizing the well-being of communities affected by industrial activities. Moreover, engaging in international collaborations and adhering to global environmental standards can enhance China's prospects for sustainability. By participating in joint ventures, sharing best practices, and embracing international environmental accords, China can demonstrate its commitment to global sustainability efforts. However, challenges persist, and navigating the complexities of sustainable development amidst rapid economic growth demands astute governance, policy coherence, and societal cooperation. Ultimately, the future prospects for sustainability within China's growth paradigm hinge on proactive measures, inclusive policies, and a resolute commitment to balancing economic progress with ecological integrity. Embracing a holistic approach that integrates environmental, social, and economic considerations is indispensable in paving the way for a sustainable future for China and the world at large.

THE U.S. ECONOMIC TRAJECTORY

OVERVIEW OF U.S. ECONOMIC PERFORMANCE: 1980 TO PRESENT

The economic performance of the United States from 1980 to the present day has been marked by a series of significant shifts and challenges. In examining major economic indicators such as GDP growth, unemployment rates, and inflation, it becomes evident that the U.S. economy has experienced both periods of robust expansion and moments of economic downturn. Throughout the 1980s, the U.S. saw substantial GDP growth driven by innovative technology, thriving industries, and increased consumer spending. However, this period was also characterized by fluctuating inflation rates and varying levels of unemployment. The country faced challenges in the form of trade deficits and high national debt. Moving into the 1990s, the U.S. witnessed a shift from a manufacturing-based economy to one increasingly dominated by services. This transition brought about changes in the composition of GDP and employment, impacting various sectors and altering the nature of work. The dot-com boom of the late 1990s fueled rapid growth, but ultimately led to the bursting of the dot-com bubble, highlighting the volatility inherent in technological advancements and their economic impact. As the 21st century unfolded, the U.S. grappled with the aftermath of the 2008 financial crisis, triggering a prolonged period of economic recovery and policy adjustments. Unemployment rates soared, while GDP growth contracted sharply, underscoring the fragility of financial markets and the interconnectedness of global economies. In recent years, the U.S. has shown signs of steady growth, albeit tempered by concerns over income inequality, trade tensions, and the management of national debt. This overview of U.S. economic performance reveals a dynamic and multifaceted landscape shaped by demographic shifts, technological innovation, and evolving global dynamics.

The Shift from Manufacturing to a Service-Oriented Economy

Over the past few decades, the United States has undergone a significant transformation in its economic structure, marked notably by the gradual decline of its manufacturing sector and the rise of a service-oriented economy. This shift has been influenced by several factors, including globalization, technological advancements, and changing consumer preferences. The traditional manufacturing-based economy, which was once the cornerstone of American industry, has gradually given way to a more diversified economic landscape dominated by services such as finance, healthcare, technology, and entertainment.

One of the primary catalysts behind this transition has been the increasing automation and mechanization of industrial processes, leading to greater efficiency and productivity in manu-facturing. While this has resulted in a reduction in labor-intensive manufacturing jobs, it has also paved the way for the expansion of the service sector, offering new employment opportunities in areas such as information technology, financial services, and telecommunications.

Furthermore, globalization and international trade have played a pivotal role in reshaping the U.S. economy. The interconnected-ness of global markets has led to the offshoring of many manu-facturing operations to countries with lower production costs, contributing to the decline of domestic manufacturing. Con-currently, the rise of emerging economies in Asia has created new export opportunities for U.S. service industries, allowing the country to capitalize on its comparative advantage in knowledge-based services.

The shift towards a service-oriented economy has also been driven by changing consumer demand. As disposable incomes have risen, there has been a corresponding increase in spending on services such as leisure, travel, and personal care. This has led to the expansion of industries catering to these growing con-sumer needs, further bolstering the prominence of the service sector in the national economy.

Despite the significant benefits of this transition, it has not been without challenges. The decline of the manufacturing sec-tor has had far-reaching socioeconomic implications, particularly in terms of job displacement and regional economic disparities. Moreover, the shift towards a service-driven economy has raised concerns about the vulnerability of the U.S. to fluctuations in consumer demand and the potential impact on employment stability.

In conclusion, the evolution from a manufacturing-centric economy to a service-oriented one reflects the dynamic nature of the U.S. economic landscape. While this shift has presented both opportunities and challenges, it underscores the adaptability and resilience of the American economy in responding to shifting global dynamics and transforming consumer preferences.

Technological Advancements and Their Impact on the Economy

Technological advancements have significantly reshaped the landscape of the U.S. economy, influencing various sectors and aspects of economic activity. The integration of advanced technologies has propelled innovation, increased productivity, and transformed business models, leading to both opportunities and challenges. One notable impact is the automation of tasks previously performed by human labor, leading to increased efficiency but also displacing certain job roles. Industries such as manufacturing, logistics, and customer service have witnessed the adoption of robotics, artificial intelligence, and data analytics, resulting in streamlined operations and enhanced precision. Additionally, technological advancements have fueled the growth of new industries such as renewable energy, biotechnology, and information technology, offering fresh opportunities for economic expansion and diversification. Digital transformation has not only revolutionized traditional businesses but has also facilitated the emergence of disruptive companies that have rapidly gained market shares. However, these advancements have given rise to concerns regarding data privacy, cybersecurity, and ethical implications of technology usage. Moreover, as the economy becomes increasingly reliant on technology, the digital divide between those with access to resources and those without has become more pronounced, raising equity issues within society. The influence of technological advancements on the economy extends beyond the private sector to government services, healthcare, education, and infrastructure. It has enabled improvements in public service delivery, medical treatments, educational outreach, and smart city initiatives. Nevertheless, it has also created a demand for a workforce equipped with digital skills and competencies, necessitating a shift in education and training programs to align with the evolving needs of the economy. Furthermore, the rapid pace of technological change has prompted discussions about the future of work, with emphasis on redefining employment dynamics and fostering adaptability among workers. As the nexus of technology and the economy continues to evolve, policymakers, businesses, and individuals must navigate these changes strategically to harness the transformative potential while mitigating associated risks. Therefore, understanding the intricate interplay between technological developments and the economy is paramount for shaping sustainable and inclusive growth in the United States.

Factors Contributing to Increasing National Debt

The escalating national debt of the United States is a complex issue stemming from various interconnected factors. One prominent determinant is the historical accumulation of deficits, often resulting from the combination of increased government spending and reduced revenue generation. The reliance on deficit financing to fund governmental operations has contributed significantly to the burgeoning national debt.

Furthermore, the cost of servicing this debt continues to rise, primarily due to the compounding effect of interest payments. As interest on the debt consumes a larger portion of the federal budget, it exerts pressure on available resources for essential public services and investments in the nation's future prosperity.

Another critical element in this equation is the impact of economic downturns and recessions, which often necessitate substantial government stimulus and relief measures. While these interventions are vital for stabilizing the economy, they can lead to an expansion of the debt as expenditures surpass revenue during challenging financial periods.

Notably, demographic shifts, particularly the aging population and increasing healthcare costs, have also played a contributory role. As the number of retirees grows and healthcare expenditure rises, the fiscal burden on the government intensifies, leading to higher spending and potentially widening deficits.

Moreover, the structure of tax policies and the administration of social welfare programs have influenced the trajectory of the national debt. Changes in tax laws, including reductions in tax rates or modifications in corporate taxation, have ramifications for government revenue, while adjustments in entitlement programs and safety nets impact expenditure patterns, both influencing the fiscal balance.

Additionally, unforeseen events such as natural disasters, pandemics, or geopolitical conflicts can necessitate emergency funding, further straining the federal budget and exacerbating the debt burden. The financial implications of these unanticipated occurrences can disrupt long-term fiscal plans and contribute to the escalation of national indebtedness.

Finally, the interplay between domestic and international economic dynamics, including trade imbalances, currency fluctuations, and global market volatility, can influence the U.S. government's borrowing requirements and debt sustainability, shaping the overall national debt landscape.

Understanding these multifaceted factors contributing to the increasing national debt provides invaluable insights for policymakers, economists, and citizens alike as they contemplate strategies to address this pressing economic challenge.

Analysis of Wage Disparities and Growing Income Inequality

Wage disparities and growing income inequality have become defining features of the American socio-economic landscape. The divergence in earnings between high-income individuals and the rest of the workforce has been steadily widening, leading to a deepening chasm in wealth distribution. This phenomenon has significant repercussions on multiple facets of society, encompassing economic stability, social cohesion, and overall well-being. To comprehend the complex dynamics at play, an exploration of the factors underpinning this inequity is crucial.

One critical element contributing to wage disparities is the transformation of the labor market due to technological advancement and globalization. While these forces have propelled overall economic growth, they have also led to the marginalization of certain segments of the workforce, particularly those engaged in routine, low-skilled tasks. The displacement of such workers has exerted downward pressure on wages in these sectors, exacerbating income differentials. Additionally, the evolution towards a service-oriented economy has resulted in a shift towards non-unionized, part-time, or contingent employment arrangements, often characterized by lower compensation and reduced benefits compared to traditional full-time positions.

Furthermore, the erosion of the real value of the federal minimum wage over the years has perpetuated income inequality. Adjusted for inflation, the federal minimum wage has markedly diminished in purchasing power, failing to keep pace with the rising cost of living. This disparity has hindered many low-wage workers from attaining financial security, perpetuating their vulnerability to socioeconomic hardships. Moreover, within corporations, executive compensation packages have surged significantly over recent decades, outstripping the pay growth of average employees. This trend can be attributed to a variety of factors, including changes in governance structures, performance-based incentives, and the increased utilization of stock options. As a result, the compensation gap between corporate leaders and frontline workers has widened dramatically, contributing to the overarching income inequality.

In light of these developments, ameliorating wage disparities and addressing growing income inequality necessitate multi-faceted strategies. Enhancing access to quality education, job training, and re-skilling initiatives can equip workers with the skills required for high-demand, well-compensated occupations, thereby mitigating income differentials. Strengthening collective bargaining rights and advocating for equitable labor policies are essential steps to uplift marginalized workers and foster more balanced income distribution within the labor force. Moreover, reassessing taxation policies to ensure progressive and fair re-distributive mechanisms can curb the concentration of wealth among the affluent while bolstering social welfare programs for low-income households. Furthermore, recalibrating corporate governance to align executive remuneration with overall em-ployee compensation can contribute to narrowing the income gap and fostering greater economic equity.

Ultimately, addressing wage disparities and income inequality demands a concerted effort from stakeholders across the public, private, and civil society spheres. By enacting comprehensive re-forms that prioritize fairness and inclusivity, the United States can forge a more equitable economic landscape, ensuring that prosperity is shared equitably among all segments of society.

Effects of Globalization on the U.S. Workforce

Globalization has significantly transformed the landscape of the U.S. workforce, bringing about both opportunities and challenges. The integration of markets and economies worldwide has led to increased competition and the free flow of capital, goods, services, and labor across borders. As a result, the U.S. workforce has witnessed several profound effects. Firstly, globalization has altered the nature of employment, with traditional manufacturing jobs being outsourced to countries with lower production costs, leading to job displacement in certain industries within the U.S. This shift has subsequently reshaped the occupational composition of the U.S. labor force, creating a greater emphasis on service-oriented and knowledge-based industries. Secondly, the influx of foreign investment and multinational corporations has introduced new technologies and work processes, necessitating a shift in the skill sets demanded by employers. The demand for highly skilled and technologically adept workers has surged, while low-skilled workers have encountered greater job insecurity and wage stagnation. Additionally, the interconnectivity of global trade has exposed the U.S. labor market to economic fluctuations and uncertainties beyond its borders, influencing employment levels and wage dynamics. Furthermore, the intensified global competition has forced U.S. businesses to adapt to rapidly changing market conditions and adopt leaner operational models, potentially impacting job stability. Moreover, the emergence of a global supply chain network has enabled businesses to leverage cost-effective production strategies, but it has also raised questions regarding labor standards, worker rights, and ethical employment practices. Notably, the impacts of globalization on the U.S. workforce extend beyond economic dimensions, encompassing social, cultural, and political ramifications. Across the nation, communities have experienced shifts in local economies, demo-graphic changes, and socio-cultural adjustments in response to global economic integration. Policymakers, industry leaders, and labor advocates are confronted with the complex task of address-ing these multifaceted challenges and opportunities posed by globalization. Hence, a nuanced understanding of the intersect-ing forces at play is essential for crafting effective policies that foster resilience, equitable opportunities, and sustainable growth for the U.S. workforce within the context of an interconnected global economy.

Government Policies and Their Role in Economic Trends

The interplay between government policies and economic trends is a crucial aspect of understanding the trajectory of any nation's economy, including that of the United States. Govern-ment policies encompass a broad range of actions and decisions taken by authorities to regulate and influence the economy's functioning. These policies can significantly impact various eco-nomic parameters such as inflation rates, employment levels, investment patterns, and overall economic growth.

Fiscal policy, involving government taxation and spending de-cisions, plays a key role in shaping economic trends. By altering tax rates and influencing public expenditure, the government can stimulate or restrain economic activities. Moreover, monetary policies, carried out by central banks, also contribute to economic trends by regulating interest rates and managing the money supply. The Federal Reserve's decisions on interest rates, for ex-ample, have far-reaching implications for investment, borrowing costs, and overall consumption within the U.S. economy.

Trade policies and international relations form another criti-cal dimension. The imposition of tariffs, trade agreements, and diplomatic ties directly influence the flow of goods and services across borders, impacting domestic industries, employment levels, and export-import dynamics. Additionally, regulatory policies in areas such as energy, healthcare, and environmental standards exert substantial influence on business operations, investment decisions, and market competitiveness.

In recent years, debates have intensified regarding the impact of government policies on income distribution and social welfare. Initiatives related to minimum wage regulations, healthcare reforms, and social security programs reflect attempts to address issues of equity and access. These policies not only affect individual households but also shape consumer behavior and aggregate demand patterns.

Furthermore, research and development (R&D) funding, education policies, and infrastructure investment are instrumental in driving long-term economic productivity and competitiveness. By fostering an environment conducive to innovation and skill development, governments play a pivotal role in setting the stage for sustainable economic growth and technological advancement.

Evaluating the effectiveness of government policies necessitates a comprehensive analysis of their intended objectives, actual outcomes, and potential unintended consequences. It also involves an understanding of the dynamic interactions among various policy measures and their combined influence on the economy. Consequently, keen attention to policy formulation and implementation becomes imperative in steering the U.S. economic trajectory towards resilience, inclusivity, and prosperity.

Retrospective Comparison with Economic Developments in China

The economic trajectory of the United States can be more comprehensively understood through a retrospective comparison with the economic developments in China. Over the past few decades, both nations have undergone significant transformations, albeit through contrasting approaches. While the U.S. has historically been a champion of free-market capitalism and has seen unparalleled technological advancements and innovation, China has rapidly emerged as a global economic powerhouse by leveraging state-led initiatives and strategic planning.

The comparative analysis reveals intriguing parallels and divergences. The U.S. economy has been characterized by its dynamic entrepreneurial spirit and emphasis on individual liberty, leading to remarkable growth in certain sectors such as technology, finance, and entertainment. Conversely, China's economic ascendance has been fueled by meticulous long-term planning and targeted investments in infrastructure, manufacturing, and human capital development, resulting in substantial gains in industrial output and export competitiveness.

As we analyze historical economic data, it becomes evident that the two nations have navigated different paths in their pursuit of economic prosperity. The U.S. has experienced periods of rapid expansion and wealth creation, often accompanied by cycles of market volatility and financial downturns. In contrast, China's centralized approach has enabled it to achieve sustained double-digit growth rates, lifting millions out of poverty and propelling the country into the forefront of global trade and investment.

Moreover, the interplay of political systems and government policies has exerted defining influences on economic outcomes in both countries. The U.S., guided by principles of democracy and limited government intervention, has fostered an environment conducive to innovation and entrepreneurship. Meanwhile, China's socialist market economy has leveraged state direction to channel resources towards strategic industries and urbanization initiatives.

Nonetheless, challenges persist in both economic models. The U.S. grapples with income inequality, mounting national debt, and disruptions caused by rapid technological advancements and globalization. Conversely, China confronts issues related to overcapacity, environmental degradation, and rebalancing its economy from investment-driven growth towards consumption-led prosperity.

Recognizing the divergent yet interconnected paths of the U.S. and China offers valuable insights into the complexities of modern economies. By studying their trajectories, policymakers, economists, and global stakeholders can gain a deeper appreciation for diverse economic paradigms and develop nuanced strategies to address contemporary challenges and harness emerging opportunities.

Current Economic Challenges and Opportunities

The current economic landscape of the United States is marked by a complex interplay of challenges and opportunities that shape its trajectory. One of the prominent challenges is the issue of wage stagnation and income inequality, which has significant implications for social stability and overall economic growth. The persistent gap between the wealthiest individuals and the rest of the population underscores the need for targeted policy interventions to address this disparity.

Another pressing challenge revolves around the rapid technological advancements and their impact on the labor market. While innovation has been a driving force behind economic growth, it has also led to workforce displacement and changes in the nature of work. Consequently, there is a growing need for upskilling and reskilling initiatives to ensure that the workforce remains adaptable and competitive in the face of automation and digitalization.

Amidst these challenges, several opportunities have emerged that have the potential to reshape the U.S. economic outlook. The transition towards renewable energy sources and sustainable practices presents a pathway for job creation and environmental preservation. By investing in clean energy infrastructure and green technologies, the nation can simultaneously address climate change and stimulate economic development.

Furthermore, the increasing interconnectedness of global markets offers opportunities for diversification and expansion. Strategic trade agreements and collaborations with emerging economies can open new avenues for U.S. businesses to tap into international demand and access resources that contribute to domestic growth.

In addition, the ongoing pursuit of research and development across various sectors fosters innovation and the emergence of new industries. This emphasis on knowledge-based economies underscores the significance of investing in education, entrepreneurship, and scientific exploration as drivers of future prosperity.

As the United States navigates through these economic challenges and explores the opportunities within its grasp, it becomes evident that effective policy formulation and strategic planning are imperative in addressing the complexities of the modern economy. Adopting a forward-looking approach that prioritizes inclusivity, sustainability, and technological advancement will position the nation to overcome challenges and leverage opportunities for long-term economic vitality.

Preparation for Understanding U.S. Debt Crisis in the Next Chapter

The impending discussion on the U.S. debt crisis is a pivotal juncture in delineating the intricacies of the nation's economic trajectory and its broader impact. To fully comprehend this multifaceted issue, it becomes imperative to delve into the historical evolution of the U.S. fiscal landscape, analyzing the catalysts that have steered the country towards its current state of indebtedness. Recognizing the interplay between domestic policies, international relations, and global economic dynamics is essential in augmenting our comprehension of the looming debt crisis. Furthermore, an in-depth exploration of the factors contributing to the escalation of national debt over time, including government expenditures, revenue generation, and fiscal management, will shed light on the underlying vulnerabilities within the U.S. financial framework. Additionally, gaining insights into the nexus between policymaking and economic resilience will enrich our understanding of the systemic issues that have predisposed the nation to the impending debt turmoil. By scrutinizing the nuanced interdependencies between debt accumulation, interest rates, and investment patterns, we can elucidate the potential ramifications and mitigative strategies pertinent to the burgeoning crisis. Moreover, juxtaposing the U.S. debt crisis alongside analogous instances from global economic history will offer a comprehensive vantage point, allowing for discerning analyses and informed projections. Embracing a multidimensional perspective, encompassing socio-political, macroeconomic, and geopolitical dimensions, will capacitate readers with the requisite acumen to engage critically with the forthcoming discourse on the U.S. debt crisis. In doing so, we are better positioned to cultivate a holistic appreciation of the complexities inherent in the U.S. economic paradigm, thereby fostering informed dialogue and strategic deliberation necessary for navigating the challenges on the horizon.

UNDERSTANDING THE U.S. DEBT CRISIS

INTRODUCTION TO U.S. NATIONAL DEBT

The U.S. national debt refers to the total amount of money that the federal government owes to its creditors. Currently, the U.S. national debt stands at over $28 trillion, representing a substantial burden on the country's economy. This figure continues to rise as the government consistently runs budget deficits, wherein its expenditures exceed its revenue. From an economic perspective, the national debt impacts various facets of the U.S. economy, including interest rates, taxation, and government spending policies.

Understanding the historical trajectory of U.S. national debt is essential in grasping its significance and long-term implications. The origins of the national debt can be traced back to the Revolutionary War and the subsequent need for financing the young nation. Over the years, significant events such as wars, economic downturns, and policy decisions have contributed to the escalation of debt levels. Notably, the national debt surged following major conflicts like World War I, World War II, and the 2008 financial crisis, reflecting the government's reliance on borrowing to fund its activities.

Evaluating the national debt from an economic standpoint requires consideration of its impact on the government's ability to finance its operations. When the government's debt rises, it competes with private sector borrowing, leading to increased interest rates that can hinder investment and economic growth. Additionally, the national debt influences fiscal policies as policy-makers are constrained in their ability to implement expansive fiscal measures due to concerns about exacerbating debt levels.

Furthermore, the level of national debt raises questions about intergenerational equity and the burden placed on future generations. By accumulating debt, the current generation benefits from government programs and services without fully bearing the financial cost, thereby passing on the obligation to repay to future taxpayers. This dynamic has profound implications for social welfare programs, infrastructure investments, and overall economic stability.

In summary, comprehending the nature and evolution of the U.S. national debt is fundamental in assessing its repercussions on the economy and society. As the national debt continues to mount, it remains a critical issue that necessitates comprehensive analysis and informed decision-making to manage its consequences effectively.

Historical Trajectory of Debt Accumulation

The historical trajectory of debt accumulation in the United States represents a complex interplay of economic, political, and social factors that have shaped the nation's fiscal landscape over centuries. It dates back to the Revolutionary War when the nascent nation first incurred debts to finance the war effort. The subsequent patterns of debt accumulation were influenced by various events such as wars, economic downturns, and evolving government policies.

Following the Civil War, the national debt soared as the government financed the reconstruction efforts and railroad expansion. However, significant progress was made during the late 19th and early 20th centuries as the U.S. experienced rapid industrial growth and fiscal discipline, enabling a steady reduction in the debt burden. This trend was abruptly interrupted by the onset of World War I, leading to a sharp spike in national debt.

The Great Depression and the New Deal era further exacerbated the debt as the government undertook expansive public works programs and social welfare initiatives to combat the economic downturn. The deficit spending continued during World War II, resulting in an unprecedented increase in the national debt. Postwar efforts led to a period of relative stability and declining debt-to-GDP ratios until the 1970s when economic challenges, along with burgeoning entitlement programs, contributed to renewed debt accumulation.

In recent decades, the national debt has been propelled by a combination of factors including tax policies, military engagements, healthcare costs, and demographic shifts. The turn of the 21st century witnessed a surge in government borrowing, partially attributed to the response to the 9/11 attacks, and a subsequent global financial crisis. The prolonged low interest rate environment following the crisis also altered the dynamics of debt accumulation.

Throughout this historical trajectory, the role of monetary policy, international trade dynamics, and geopolitical considerations has been pivotal in influencing the ebb and flow of the national debt. Understanding this historical context provides crucial insights into the complexities of managing and addressing the contemporary challenges associated with U.S. debt accumulation.

Major Foreign Creditors and Their Impact

As the United States government continues to accumulate debt, the role of major foreign creditors has become increasingly significant in shaping the national economic landscape. Countries such as China and Japan hold substantial portions of U.S. Treasury securities, thus wielding considerable influence over U.S. fiscal policies and international financial dynamics.

China, in particular, stands out as one of the largest foreign holders of U.S. debt. Its extensive investments in U.S. Treasury bonds have sparked discussions and debates regarding the potential leverage that China could exert over the U.S. economy. The sheer scale of China's holdings prompts considerations about how its actions may impact U.S. interest rates, currency values, and overall economic stability. Similarly, Japan's sizable ownership of U.S. debt instruments lends weight to its involvement in shaping American economic decisions.

The reliance on foreign creditors presents both opportunities and risks for the United States. On the one hand, it allows the government to secure necessary funding for various initiatives and projects. However, this dependence also leaves the nation vulnerable to external influences, potentially compromising its financial independence and sovereignty. The intricate interplay between the U.S. and its major foreign creditors underscores the complexities of global financial interconnectedness and underscores the necessity of prudent debt management strategies.

Furthermore, the actions and policies of these major foreign creditors can significantly impact not only the U.S. economy but also the broader global financial system. The decisions made by these creditors, whether related to holdings, divestitures, or trade arrangements, reverberate across international markets, influencing exchange rates, investment patterns, and overall economic sentiments. Therefore, understanding their impact is pivotal for policymakers, economists, and market participants alike, as it directly affects strategic economic planning and risk assessments.

In assessing the implications of major foreign creditors on the U.S. debt crisis, it is crucial to recognize the need for balanced and nuanced perspectives. While acknowledging the potential challenges posed by significant external ownership of U.S. debt, it is also essential to identify opportunities for cooperative engagement and mutual benefit. The delicate balance between leveraging foreign investments for economic growth and mitigating vulnerability to external pressures requires careful navigation and thoughtful policy formulation.

Debt Instruments Utilized by the U.S. Government

The U.S. government utilizes a variety of debt instruments to finance its operations and manage the national debt. Treasury securities, including Treasury bills (T-bills), Treasury notes, and Treasury bonds, are among the primary debt instruments issued by the U.S. Department of the Treasury. These securities play a crucial role in borrowing funds from the public, financial institutions, and foreign governments to meet the government's financing needs. Treasury bills are short-term securities with maturities ranging from a few days to one year, making them an essential tool for meeting short-term borrowing requirements. Treasury notes have maturities ranging from two to ten years, while Treasury bonds have maturities of more than ten years, allowing the government to manage long-term funding needs. These instruments are sold at public auctions and can also be purchased in the secondary market. Moreover, savings bonds, which are non-marketable securities, represent another form of debt instrument used by the U.S. government to raise funds directly from individual investors. The Series EE and Series I savings bonds are examples of these debt instruments that provide a safe and accessible means of investing in the nation's debt. Additionally, the government issues inflation-protected securities known as Treasury Inflation-Protected Securities (TIPS) to protect investors from inflation risk. TIPS provide investors with a hedge against inflation and ensure that their returns maintain purchasing power over time. Lastly, the U.S. government also utilizes federal agency and government-sponsored enterprise securities to finance specific sectors, such as housing and agriculture, through agencies like Fannie Mae and Freddie Mac. These debt instruments contribute to the diverse toolkit employed by the U.S. government to effectively manage the national debt and support various sectors of the economy.

Role of Treasury Bonds in National Debt

The issuance of treasury bonds by the U.S. government plays a pivotal role in the national debt dynamics. Treasury bonds, also known as T-bonds, are long-term debt securities with maturities ranging from 10 to 30 years, and they are regarded as one of the safest investment options due to the backing of the full faith and credit of the U.S. government. These bonds serve as integral components of the broader U.S. debt profile, allowing the government to finance various projects and initiatives. Moreover, treasury bonds form a significant part of the total outstanding public debt, exerting a substantial influence on the overall fiscal health and economic stability of the nation. The issuance and management of these bonds carry profound implications for the functioning of financial markets, monetary policy, and investor sentiment.

Treasury bonds serve as fundamental instruments for the government to raise capital from investors, including domestic and foreign entities, to fund federal expenditures and bridge budgetary shortfalls. By issuing these bonds, the government effectively borrows funds from the public, providing investors with a secure avenue to allocate their capital while earning fixed interest income over the bond's tenure. This mechanism enables the government to meet its funding requirements, address immediate cash needs, and execute key programs without solely relying on revenues or additional taxation. The flexibility offered by treasury bonds in sourcing capital is particularly vital during periods of economic downturns, emergencies, or when substantial investments in infrastructure, defense, or social welfare are essential.

Furthermore, the active trading of treasury bonds in the secondary market significantly influences the broader financial landscape. The yields on these bonds serve as crucial benchmarks for various other interest rates, impacting borrowing costs for businesses, consumers, and state and local governments. Additionally, the demand and supply dynamics of treasury bonds can signal prevailing market sentiments, the outlook on inflation, and overall confidence in the U.S. economy. As a result, the performance of treasury bonds is closely monitored by economists, policymakers, and investors as an indicator of the government's creditworthiness, monetary conditions, and macroeconomic trends.

In summary, treasury bonds play a multifaceted role within the fabric of the national debt, intertwining with fiscal, monetary, and investment domains. Their issuance not only facilitates government funding but also reverberates across financial markets and macroeconomic landscapes. A comprehensive understanding of the intricacies surrounding treasury bonds is imperative for assessing the dynamics of U.S. debt sustainability, financial market behavior, and economic resilience.

Influence of Debt on Fiscal Policy

The influence of national debt on fiscal policy is a topic of paramount importance within the realm of economic governance. As the U.S. continues to grapple with mounting debt levels, the impact on fiscal policy cannot be understated. Elevated national debt imposes significant constraints on the government's ability to implement and sustain effective fiscal policies for economic stability and growth. In this context, it becomes imperative to analyze the interplay between escalating debt burdens and the formulation of fiscal policies that are instrumental in shaping the nation's economic trajectory.

Long-Term Effects on Economic Growth and Stability

The long-term implications of the U.S. national debt on economic growth and stability are complex and multifaceted. As the national debt continues to escalate, there are various interconnected factors that come into play, influencing the broader economic landscape. One crucial aspect pertains to the impact on interest rates and investment. The accumulation of national debt can lead to increased demand for borrowing, causing upward pressure on interest rates. Elevated interest rates subsequently translate into higher borrowing costs for businesses and consumers alike. This, in turn, could deter investment and ultimately curtail economic growth. Moreover, mounting national debt is likely to result in greater reliance on foreign entities for financing. Such reliance raises concerns about the country's economic sovereignty and vulnerability to external economic shocks and geopolitical dynamics. Additionally, the burden of servicing the national debt can divert substantial resources away from critical areas such as infrastructure development, education, and healthcare, which are vital for fostering long-term economic growth and stability. Another pertinent consideration is the intergenerational impact of the burgeoning national debt. As the debt accumulates, future generations may be saddled with the responsibility of repaying or managing it. This could potentially limit their fiscal flexibility and erode their standard of living. Furthermore, a high national debt-to-GDP ratio has the potential to hinder government initiatives aimed at stimulating the economy during periods of downturn or recession. The presence of a large debt burden constrains the government's capacity to enact counter-cyclical policies, thereby impeding efforts to mitigate economic downturns. Beyond this, a growing national debt may contribute to a loss of confidence in the economy among both domestic and international stakeholders, leading to reduced investments, heightened market volatility, and diminished long-term prosperity. In conclusion, the long-term effects of the U.S. national debt on economic growth and stability extend far beyond fiscal considerations. They encompass repercussions across multiple domains, including interest rates, investment, national sovereignty, intergenerational equity, and the government's ability to respond to economic challenges. Addressing the national debt is paramount to securing a sustainable and prosperous economic future for the United States and its citizens.

Implications for Future Generations

As we grapple with the complexity of the U.S. debt crisis, it is crucial to acknowledge the profound implications that this burden will impose on future generations. The national debt not only reflects our current fiscal policies but also serves as an ominous legacy that will significantly impact the economic landscape for our descendants. The accumulation of debt places an immense financial strain on future generations, threatening their prospects for sustained prosperity and well-being.

The pervasive influence of burgeoning debt cannot be underestimated. First and foremost, the escalating national debt exerts upward pressure on interest rates, thereby constraining the government's ability to allocate resources toward critical public services, infrastructure development, and social welfare programs. This predicament engenders a troubling dynamic in which future generations are forced to bear the weight of interest payments, perpetuating a cycle of constrained fiscal flexibility and limited governmental responsiveness to emerging societal needs.

Another pressing concern pertains to the diminishing capacity for future policymakers to effectively respond to unanticipated economic shocks. The ballooning national debt curtails the extent to which discretionary fiscal policy can be effectively leveraged as a countercyclical tool during periods of economic downturn. Consequently, the hands of future leaders may be shackled, limiting their ability to mitigate the impact of recessions, bolster employment, and catalyze sustainable growth.

Moreover, the accrued national debt undermines the intergenerational equity that underpins socio-economic progress. By deferring a significant portion of current expenditures onto future generations, we perpetuate a form of intertemporal inequity that compromises the egalitarian ethos of our society. Should the debt remain unchecked, the ensuing burden could transmute into heightened tax liabilities or diminished access to essential public goods for our progeny, thereby exacerbating societal disparities and impeding social mobility.

Amid these foreboding implications, it becomes imperative to contemplate strategies that can ameliorate the looming perils entailed by the national debt. Through prudent fiscal reforms, thoughtful allocation of resources, and proactive debt management, we can strive to alleviate the magnitude of this burden and mitigate its adverse implications for the prosperity of generations yet to come. However, such initiatives necessitate a concerted and sustained commitment to fostering fiscal responsibility and safeguarding the economic destinies of our posterity.

Debt Management Strategies

Amidst the intricate web of economic challenges posed by the U.S. national debt, an in-depth exploration of viable debt management strategies becomes imperative. Recognizing that the implications of unsustainable debt transcend current generations, strategic measures must be employed to navigate through these turbulent fiscal waters. One approach revolves around proactive fiscal policies aimed at deficit reduction through a combination of revenue enhancement and spending reforms. As Congress grapples with the complex task of addressing the national debt, a transparent and bipartisan commitment to long-term fiscal sustainability emerges as a central tenet. This involves reevaluating tax structures, entitlement programs, and discretionary spending, while fostering economic growth to stabilize the debt-to-GDP ratio. Another critical aspect pertains to prudent debt restructuring, where the government seeks to optimize its financial obligations by refinancing existing debt at lower interest rates or extending maturities to alleviate immediate repayment pressures. Furthermore, fostering domestic savings and channeling them into productive investments can curtail reliance on foreign creditors, thereby reinforcing the nation's fiscal sovereignty. Embracing innovative financial instruments and incentive mechanisms to promote national saving while reducing public borrowing envisages a pathway towards sustainable debt levels. Leveraging comprehensive risk-assessment frameworks and stress testing methodologies can refine debt management practices, ensuring resilience against external shocks and market volatilities. Additionally, enhancing coordination and collaboration among federal agencies, regulatory bodies, and monetary authorities can harmonize debt management efforts, fostering a coherent and integrated approach. Embracing forward-looking transparency practices ensures that both policymakers and the public are well-informed about the trajectory of the national debt, laying the groundwork for informed decision-making and effective public discourse. Empowering citizens with a profound understanding of the complexities surrounding the national debt engenders a collective sense of responsibility and awareness, anchoring them as integral stakeholders in the pursuit of fiscal stability. Adopting a holistic approach that transcends political divides and embraces technocratic expertise is vital to navigating the myriad challenges associated with managing the national debt. Ultimately, recognizing the interconnected nature of the global financial landscape and collaborating with international partners to harmonize debt management initiatives fosters a unified front against systemic vulnerabilities. In sum, a multi-faceted approach blending fiscal prudence, innovative strategies, and proactive institutional frameworks forms the bedrock for efficacious debt management in safeguarding the future prosperity of the United States.

Conclusion: Pathways to Mitigating Debt Challenges

As the world's largest economy, the United States faces significant challenges in managing its national debt. To mitigate these challenges, a multifaceted approach is essential. Firstly, promoting fiscal discipline and responsible spending practices within the government is paramount. This requires a comprehensive review of public expenditures, with a focus on prioritizing investments that yield long-term economic benefits while minimizing non-essential outlays. Moreover, enhancing revenue generation through a fair and efficient tax system is vital to address budget shortfalls without exacerbating the burden on taxpayers.

Additionally, fostering economic growth through strategic policies can bolster the government's capacity to service its debt obligations. By investing in critical infrastructure, technology, and innovation, the U.S. can stimulate productivity gains and nurture sustainable development, thereby expanding the tax base and reducing reliance on borrowing. Furthermore, implementing measures to address structural issues such as income inequality and healthcare costs is essential for fortifying the overall fiscal health of the nation.

In parallel, diplomatic efforts should be undertaken to cultivate constructive relationships with key foreign creditors. Open communication and cooperation are imperative to instill confidence and stability in the global financial landscape, mitigating the risk of sudden capital flight or adverse adjustments in interest rates. Through dialogue and collaboration, the U.S. can proactively manage its debt exposure and cultivate a favorable environment for sustained economic prosperity.

Moreover, embracing prudent debt management strategies, such as refinancing existing debt at favorable terms and diversifying funding sources, can help ameliorate the associated financial risks. An adept utilization of financial instruments, including

Treasury bonds, warrants careful consideration to optimize the cost and maturity profile of the debt portfolio. Additionally, instituting transparent reporting mechanisms and enacting legislation to enforce responsible borrowing practices are pivotal in safeguarding against unchecked accumulation of national debt.

Ultimately, a collective commitment to addressing the U.S. debt crisis necessitates bipartisan consensus and a long-term perspective. Political leaders, policymakers, and citizens must collaborate to confront the complex challenge of managing the national debt. By charting a course marked by fiscal responsibility, sustainable economic growth, and international cooperation, the United States can navigate the path towards mitigating debt challenges, ensuring its enduring fiscal stability and prosperity for future generations.

THE 2008 FINANCIAL CRISIS AND BEYOND

Introduction to the 2008 Financial Crisis

The financial crisis of 2008 is widely regarded as one of the most significant economic events in modern history, reshaping the global financial landscape and profoundly impacting economies on a global scale. Prior to delving into an in-depth analysis of this pivotal period, it is essential to provide a comprehensive overview that contextualizes the circumstances leading up to the crisis. The years preceding 2008 were characterized by a period of economic exuberance, with the United States experiencing robust growth, buoyant consumer spending, and rapidly expanding credit markets. Concurrently, a housing boom fueled by lax lending standards and financial innovation swept across the nation, creating an illusion of prosperity. The era was also marked by a proliferation of complex financial products, such as mortgage-backed securities and collateralized debt obligations, which amplified the exposure of banks and investors to subprime mortgages. Amidst this apparent economic vigor, warning signs began to emerge, albeit overlooked by many. The rapid escalation of housing prices, coupled with an insatiable demand for mortgage-backed securities, masked underlying vulnerabilities within the financial system. Additionally, financial institutions engaged in reckless risk-taking behaviors, leveraging their capital to unprecedented levels and creating a fragile interconnected web of financial interdependencies. This environment of overconfidence and complacency ultimately set the stage for the imminent upheaval. As we delve deeper into the intricacies of the 2008 financial crisis, it becomes imperative to unravel the labyrinth of factors that culminated in the tumultuous events of that year, shedding light on the intricate series of catalysts that precipitated the onset of the crisis and its profound ramifications.

Overview of the U.S. Economic Climate Pre-2008

Prior to the 2008 financial crisis, the United States experienced a period of economic growth and prosperity that was marked by several key developments. The late 20th century saw the U.S. economy undergo significant transformations, including the rise of technology, globalization of trade, and deregulation of financial markets. These factors contributed to an environment characterized by rapid expansion, increased consumer spending, and booming asset prices. The housing market, in particular, experienced unprecedented growth, fueled by low interest rates and relaxed lending standards. This led to a surge in homeownership and a perception of perpetually rising property values. Additionally, the financial sector underwent substantial changes, with the proliferation of complex financial instruments and the emergence of new forms of risk-taking. As a result, the country experienced a prolonged period of low volatility and seemingly endless economic opportunity. However, beneath this façade of prosperity, there were underlying vulnerabilities that would ultimately lead to the catastrophic events of 2008. The combination of excessive risk-taking, inflated asset prices, unsustainable debt levels, and insufficient regulatory oversight set the stage for the impending crisis. While the immediate pre-crisis years were marked by apparent economic success, they also sowed the seeds of a tumultuous and far-reaching downturn that would have profound implications for the global economy. Understanding the dynamics of the U.S. economic climate prior to 2008 is essential for comprehending the context in which the financial crisis unfolded and for formulating strategies to prevent similar crises in the future.

Key Causes of the 2008 Financial Crisis

The 2008 financial crisis, also known as the Global Financial Crisis (GFC), was one of the most severe economic downturns in modern history with far-reaching implications for global economies. Several key factors converged to create the perfect storm that led to this catastrophic event. Understanding these causes is crucial to grasping the complexities of the crisis and its aftermath. One of the primary catalysts was the housing market bubble, fueled by lax lending standards, low interest rates, and a surge in subprime mortgage lending. Financial institutions bundled these risky mortgages into complex securities which were then marketed globally. As the housing bubble burst, the value of these securities plummeted, triggering widespread panic and distrust in the financial markets. Additionally, regulatory failures and inadequate oversight allowed for the proliferation of risky financial products and unsustainable leverage within the banking system. This lack of regulation contributed significantly to the crisis. Furthermore, the interconnected nature of global financial systems amplified the impact of the crisis. With the increasing intertwining of international banks and financial institutions, the shockwaves from the U.S. housing market reverberated worldwide, undermining stability across diverse economies. The over-reliance on credit rating agencies for risk assessment also played a pivotal role. These agencies failed to accurately evaluate the true risks associated with mortgage-backed securities, leading investors to misjudge the safety of these investments. Lastly, the absence of effective risk management practices within financial institutions exacerbated the crisis. Many firms grossly underestimated their exposure to the collapsing housing market and lacked the necessary liquidity to weather the storm. Ultimately, a combination of these factors created a systemic crisis that brought the global financial system to the brink of collapse, impacting millions of individuals and businesses worldwide.

Immediate Effects on Global Financial Markets

The 2008 financial crisis sent shockwaves through global financial markets, triggering a domino effect of unprecedented proportions. As the crisis unfolded, stock markets plummeted, credit markets froze, and investor confidence reached historic lows. The interconnectedness of the global economy meant that no market or country was immune to the turmoil, leading to a synchronized downturn across major financial hubs. The contagion effect rapidly spread from the epicenter in the United States to Europe, Asia, and beyond, wreaking havoc on both developed and emerging economies. Central banks and regulatory authorities scrambled to contain the fallout, injecting liquidity into the system and implementing emergency measures to stabilize disrupted markets. However, the severity and swiftness of the crisis caught many off guard, revealing the vulnerabilities of interconnected global financial systems. As investors fled riskier assets for safe havens, commodities and currencies experienced extreme volatility, exacerbating the turmoil. Uncertainty dominated trading floors, with fear and panic gripping market participants, leading to massive sell-offs and destabilizing asset price movements. The once reliable and robust financial instruments were suddenly devalued, triggering a crisis of confidence and a loss of faith in the stability of the global financial architecture. The realization that institutions deemed 'too big to fail' were indeed vulnerable sent shockwaves through Wall Street and beyond, leading to a reevaluation of risk assessment and management practices. Amid the chaos, the interconnected and interdependent nature of global financial markets became glaringly apparent, highlighting the need for international cooperation and unified responses during times of crisis. The immediate effects on global financial markets reverberated around the world, serving as a wake-up call to the risks inherent in an increasingly interconnected and complex financial landscape.

Impact on Real Economy and Employment Figures

The impact of the 2008 financial crisis on the real economy and employment figures was substantial and far-reaching. As financial institutions collapsed and credit markets froze, the effects cascaded through the broader economy, leading to a severe contraction in economic activity. The crisis triggered a sharp decline in consumer spending and business investment, as uncertainty and a lack of credit availability forced both individuals and companies to cut back on their expenditures. This, in turn, led to a steep drop in production and output across various industries, exacerbating the economic downturn. Unemployment rates soared as businesses struggled to stay afloat amidst the tumultuous environment, resulting in significant job losses that reverberated throughout communities nationwide. The labor market faced a prolonged period of distress, with job seekers finding it increasingly difficult to secure employment, compounding the challenges posed by the recession. Many individuals experienced prolonged spells of unemployment, leading to financial hardships, increased stress, and damage to their long-term career prospects. Moreover, the housing market collapse intensified the crisis, contributing to widespread foreclosures, declining property values, and diminished household wealth, thereby further impacting consumer confidence and spending. The overall effect on households was profound, leading to reduced disposable income, savings depletion, and heightened anxiety about the future. Small businesses, a vital component of the economy, faced unprecedented hurdles, with many being forced to shut down or drastically downsize, leading to a loss of entrepreneurial spirit and local job opportunities. The crisis laid bare the interconnectedness of the financial system with the real economy, exposing vulnerabilities that had been underestimated or overlooked. Policy responses to address the fallout from the crisis were multifaceted, aimed at stabilizing financial markets, reigniting economic growth, and tackling unemployment. However, the scars left by the crisis continued to linger, necessitating sustained efforts to address the enduring impact on individuals, businesses, and the broader socioeconomic fabric.

Government Interventions: Responses and Bailouts

In response to the 2008 financial crisis, the U.S. government implemented various interventions aiming to mitigate the negative impacts on financial institutions and stabilize the economy. One significant measure was the Troubled Asset Relief Program (TARP), a $700 billion initiative that aimed to purchase distressed assets and equity from financial institutions to strengthen the financial sector. This program helped prevent the collapse of several major banks and financial organizations, thereby averting a potentially catastrophic domino effect.

Additionally, the Federal Reserve employed expansionary monetary policy, lowering interest rates and initiating quantitative easing to provide liquidity to financial markets and stimulate economic activity. The government also intervened in the automotive industry, offering bailouts to prevent the collapse of major automakers such as General Motors and Chrysler, which were integral to the broader manufacturing sector and employment landscape.

The regulatory landscape witnessed significant changes in the aftermath of the crisis. The Dodd-Frank Wall Street Reform and Consumer Protection Act of 2010 represented a comprehensive overhaul of financial regulation, aiming to address the vulnerabilities and practices that had contributed to the crisis. The legislation introduced measures such as stricter capital requirements, enhanced oversight of derivatives markets, the establishment of the Consumer Financial Protection Bureau, and the implementation of the Volcker Rule to restrict proprietary trading by banks.

Critics argued that the government interventions and bailouts created moral hazard, incentivizing risky behavior by financial institutions under the assumption of future government support. However, proponents countered that the immediate stabilization and avoidance of a deeper economic downturn justified these actions. The debate surrounding the effectiveness and consequences of these interventions continues to be a prominent topic in economic discussions, with ongoing implications for future crisis management strategies.

As the global financial system evolves, understanding the repercussions and outcomes of these interventions becomes increasingly critical. The efficacy of government responses and bailouts in stabilizing the economy and preventing systemic collapse serves as a cornerstone in shaping future regulatory frameworks and crisis management policies.

Lessons Learned and Regulatory Changes

Following the catastrophic consequences of the 2008 financial crisis, governments and regulatory bodies around the world embarked on widespread introspection, aiming to identify the critical flaws in the financial systems that had precipitated the meltdown. At the forefront of this exercise was the United States, whose economy had been at the epicenter of the crisis. In response to the calamity, Congress implemented a series of legislative reforms intended to address the inadequacies in the financial regulatory framework. The Dodd-Frank Wall Street Reform and Consumer Protection Act, signed into law in July 2010, represented the most comprehensive overhaul of financial regulation in the U.S. since the Great Depression. This landmark legislation aimed to enhance accountability and transparency within the financial industry by imposing stricter regulations on banks, hedge funds, and other financial institutions. Additionally, it established the Consumer Financial Protection Bureau to safeguard consumers from predatory lending and deceptive financial practices. Moreover, it sought to curb systemic risk by introducing provisions for the orderly liquidation of failing financial firms and the creation of the Financial Stability Oversight Council to monitor potential threats to the stability of the financial system. The aftermath of the crisis also prompted the Financial Accounting Standards Board to revise accounting standards, promoting greater transparency in corporate financial reporting. Furthermore, governing bodies across the globe collaborated to enhance international coordination on financial regulation through initiatives such as the Basel III framework. By revamping capital requirements and fostering stricter risk management practices, global policymakers endeavored to fortify the resilience of financial institutions against future shocks. Despite these significant reforms, criticism emerged regarding the efficacy of certain regulations and the unintended consequences they posed. Accordingly, ongoing debates continue to shape the regulatory environment, emphasizing the perpetual challenge of maintaining an optimal balance between financial stability, innovation, and economic growth.

Ongoing Vulnerabilities in the U.S. Financial System

The 2008 financial crisis prompted significant regulatory changes and introspection within the U.S. financial system. However, despite these measures, there remain ongoing vulnerabilities that pose potential risks to the stability of the financial system. One key vulnerability lies in the interconnectedness of financial institutions. The integration of global financial markets means that the failure of a major institution could have far-reaching implications, as evidenced by the ripple effects of the collapse of Lehman Brothers in 2008. Additionally, the prevalence of complex financial products such as derivatives and structured securities continues to present challenges in assessing and managing risk. These instruments can obscure the true level of risk exposure for financial institutions and investors, potentially leading to systemic issues in times of market stress. Moreover, the persistence of too-big-to-fail institutions poses a continued risk. While efforts have been made to bolster capital requirements and implement stringent stress testing, the sheer size and influence of these institutions mean that their potential failure could still destabilize the financial system. Another vulnerability lies in the evolving nature of cyber threats. Technological advancements have facilitated greater efficiency and connectivity within the financial sector, but they have also exposed it to new risks. Cyber attacks targeting financial infrastructure, data breaches, and ransomware threats continue to pose a grave danger, given the heavy reliance on digital systems and networks for critical financial operations. Furthermore, the prolonged low interest rate environment has led to concerns about the potential misallocation of capital and unsustainable asset price inflation. The search for yield in a low-rate environment has driven investors towards riskier assets and highly leveraged investment strategies, which could exacerbate instability in the event of an economic downturn. Addressing these vulnerabilities is crucial for ensuring the resilience of the U.S. financial system. Policymakers, regulators, and industry participants must continue to collaborate in monitoring and addressing these risks through enhanced oversight, stress testing, and the implementation of robust risk management practices. Moreover, international cooperation is essential, given the interconnectedness of global financial systems. By staying vigilant and proactive in identifying and mitigating vulnerabilities, the U.S. financial system can better withstand future challenges and contribute to the overall stability of the world economy.

Predicting and Mitigating Future Crises

Financial crises are complex events that arise from a multitude of interrelated factors, making their prediction inherently challenging. However, certain indicators can serve as warning signs for potential future crises. To mitigate the risk and impact of such crises, policymakers, financial institutions, and regulators must be vigilant in monitoring these indicators and implementing proactive measures. One key area of focus is the assessment of systemic risk within the financial system. This involves analyzing the interconnectedness of financial institutions, the prevalence of leverage, and the exposure to risky assets. Additionally, monitoring indicators such as rapid credit growth, asset price bubbles, and excessive risk-taking behavior can provide valuable insights into potential vulnerabilities. Moreover, stress testing various scenarios can help assess the resilience of the financial system to adverse shocks. In parallel, enhancing transparency and disclosure requirements for financial institutions can improve market discipline and risk management. Strengthening regulatory frameworks and supervisory oversight is crucial in mitigating future crises. This entails implementing robust capital and liquidity requirements, designing effective resolution mechanisms for troubled institutions, and enhancing risk management standards. Furthermore, leveraging advancements in technology and data analytics can aid in the early detection of emerging risks and the rapid response to potential threats. Collaboration between domestic and international regulatory bodies is essential in addressing global interconnectedness and cross-border spillover effects. The coordination of macroprudential policies and the harmonization of regulatory standards can contribute to a more resilient and stable global financial system. Proactive measures should also extend to the realm of monetary policy. Central banks play a pivotal role in preserving financial stability, and they must carefully balance their objectives of price stability and systemic risk management. Maintaining a forward-looking approach to monetary policy and adopting a comprehensive macrofinancial perspective can help identify imbalances and proactively address emerging vulnerabilities. Finally, fostering a culture of risk awareness and responsible decision-making within financial institutions is paramount. Encouraging a long-term orientation, robust risk governance frameworks, and ethical conduct can instill greater resilience and reduce the likelihood of excessive risk-taking behavior. By embracing a multifaceted approach that encompasses macroprudential regulation, monetary policy, systemic risk assessment, and industry best practices, stakeholders can collectively strive towards a more stable and resilient financial system, better equipped to predict and mitigate future crises.

Conclusion: Implications for U.S.-China Economic Relations

The interconnectedness of the global economy means that the implications of the 2008 financial crisis extend far beyond the borders of the United States. As we have explored in this book, one of the most critical dimensions of these implications revolves around the economic relationship between the United States and China. The two largest economies in the world share a complex and multifaceted interdependence, with significant impacts on the stability and growth of both nations.

The 2008 financial crisis underscored the extent to which the U.S. and Chinese economies are linked. The crisis served as a wake-up call, emphasizing the need for enhanced collaboration and communication between the two economic powerhouses. It has become clear that sustainable economic development and global financial stability heavily depend on how the U.S. and China manage their economic relations.

Moving forward, it is imperative for both countries to prioritize open dialogue, transparent trade policies, and mutually beneficial agreements. Proactive efforts must be made to address trade imbalances, currency valuation concerns, and intellectual property rights protection. Moreover, building trust through continued engagement and shared responsibility will be vital in navigating future economic challenges.

Furthermore, with the rise of economic nationalism and protectionist tendencies, it is essential for the U.S. and China to resist the temptation of isolationism and instead embrace a cooperative approach. By working together to harness each other's strengths and mitigate weaknesses, both nations can contribute to fostering global economic stability and prosperity.

This chapter has highlighted the intricate web of U.S.-China economic relations, underscoring the importance of fostering an environment that encourages productive collaboration and healthy competition. As the global economic landscape evolves, the actions and decisions made by both countries will continue to reverberate across the world. Ultimately, the implications for U.S.-China economic relations go beyond bilateral interests; they hold profound significance for the future of the global economy.

ECONOMIC INTERDEPENDENCE BETWEEN THE U.S. AND CHINA

INTRODUCTION TO U.S.-CHINA ECONOMIC RELATIONS

The economic relations between the United States and China have evolved significantly since the 1970s, marking a pivotal point in global economics. As two of the world's largest economies, their engagements have reverberated through the international economic landscape, shaping and redefining the dynamics of globalization. What originated as cautious and tentative interactions has developed into an intricate web of interdependence, encompassing trade, investment, and financial ties.

Post-1970s, the normalization of diplomatic relations between the U.S. and China laid the groundwork for burgeoning economic cooperation. This period witnessed the establishment of various bilateral agreements and trade pacts, fostering the exchange of goods, services, and technology. The U.S.-China economic relations have not only facilitated immense trade flows but also engendered cross-border investment, technological collaborations, and joint ventures, amplifying commercial synergies and opportunities for prosperity.

Contemporary issues in U.S.-China economic relations loom large on the global stage, influencing geopolitical strategies and market dynamics. The prevalence of complex trade disputes, intellectual property conflicts, and strategic techno-economic competition underscores the multifaceted nature of their entwined economic relationship. Moreover, debates on currency manipulation, market access, and regulatory disparities continue to shape the course of their economic engagements, resonating with wider implications for global economic governance.

In the realms of finance and investment, the U.S.-China economic entanglement is further underscored by the intricate mesh of financial linkages. The magnitude of U.S. debt holdings by China, along with the intricacies of financial markets, adds an extra layer of complexity to their interdependent economic nexus. These factors collectively contribute to accentuating the symbiotic nature of their economic relations and the significant impact they exert on the global economic order.

The evolving and intricate nature of U.S.-China economic relations serves as a reflector of the changing tides in global economics. Understanding this dynamic interplay is imperative for navigating the contemporary economic landscape, especially considering its far-reaching consequences and the potential to shape the future trajectory of global economic governance.

The Architect of Debt: Historical Overview

Throughout the course of history, the economic relationship between the United States and China has undergone significant transformations. To truly understand the depth and complexity of their current financial interdependence, it is essential to delve into the historical roots that have shaped this intricate partnership. The mid-20th century saw a pivotal shift in global economic dynamics, with the United States emerging as a leading superpower after World War II. This period marked the onset of significant economic ties between the U.S. and China, albeit in a largely indirect manner due to geopolitical constraints. It wasn't until the latter part of the 20th century that diplomatic relations between the two nations began to thaw, opening the floodgates for expanded economic collaboration. The onset of globalization further propelled this economic entwinement, as trade and investment between the U.S. and China surged dramatically. However, this burgeoning economic alliance was not without its challenges. Structural disparities, ideological differences, and geopolitical tensions created a complex backdrop against which economic relations unfolded. The catalyst for the skyrocketing U.S. debt to China lay in a confluence of factors, including massive trade imbalances, evolving global supply chains, and shifting comparative advantages. As the U.S. grappled with internal economic upheavals, such as the 2008 financial crisis, its debt burden burgeoned, much of which was financed by China. This historical context serves as a crucial lens through which we can comprehensively dissect the nature and implications of the present-day economic interdependence between these two global powerhouses. Unraveling the historical threads woven into the fabric of U.S.-China economic relations allows us to gain insightful perspectives on the striking intricacies and potential future trajectories of this indispensable partnership.

Analysis of the Current U.S. Debt to China

The complex web of economic interdependence between the United States and China has been intricately woven over the past several decades. Central to this relationship is the substantial amount of U.S. debt held by China, which has profound implications for both nations and their global standing. A meticulous analysis of the current U.S. debt to China reveals a dynamic and multi-faceted situation that warrants close examination. The sheer size of the U.S. debt, combined with China's status as a major creditor, underscores the intricate nature of their financial entanglement. It's imperative to delve into the composition of this debt, considering both its short-term and long-term implications. Additionally, factors such as interest rates, repayment terms, and the strategic use of U.S. treasuries by China shape the complexity of this relationship. In essence, the extent and nature of the U.S. debt to China necessitates a comprehensive review of the associated risks, as well as the potential benefits for both countries. Moreover, an exploration of the power dynamics inherent in this financial arrangement sheds light on how it influences broader geopolitical relations. As such, a nuanced understanding of the current U.S. debt to China offers valuable insights into the intricate interplay of economics, politics, and global influence. Only through such an analysis can we truly appreciate the magnitude of this complex financial connection.

Mechanisms of Economic Leverage in Bilateral Relations

Economic leverage between the United States and China is a complex web interwoven with financial, political, and strategic considerations. As the two largest economies on the global stage, their bilateral relations are profoundly influential, shaping not only their own economic trajectories but also reverberating across the international economic landscape. Within this intricate tapestry of economic interdependence lie a multitude of mechanisms through which both nations exert leverage and negotiate power dynamics.

One critical mechanism is trade dependence, where each country's reliance on the other for imports and exports creates a form of inherent leverage. China's significant role as a major exporter to the U.S. establishes a level of economic control while the U.S.'s imports from China provide a crucial source of demand for Chinese goods. Moreover, foreign direct investment (FDI) acts as another key lever, with both nations using investments to establish economic ties and influence industrial sectors and technological advancement.

Financial instruments such as currency exchange rates and monetary policy also play a pivotal role in exercising economic leverage. The value of the Chinese yuan against the U.S. dollar and vice versa can significantly impact trade balances and fiscal policies. Additionally, the management of sovereign debt holdings and issuance provides further avenues for leveraging interdependence, shaping decisions on interest rates, creditworthiness, and capital flows.

Beyond these economic aspects, geopolitical considerations form a significant part of the leverage equation. Soft power tools in the form of diplomacy, cultural influences, and international alliances serve as levers through which both countries engage in a subtle dance of power projection and economic influence. Not to be overlooked, technology access and innovation capabilities further underpin the complexity of economic leverage, with both nations vying for dominance in industries and technological breakthroughs that will shape the future global economy.

The intricacy of these mechanisms illuminates the multi-dimensionality of the U.S.-China economic relationship. It offers a window into the strategic calculations, negotiations, and power dynamics that define their bilateral ties, presenting a kaleidoscope of interconnected interests, influences, and implications that ripple far beyond their national borders.

Debt Dynamics: Geostrategic Implications

The intertwining of debt between the United States and China has far-reaching geostrategic implications that extend beyond the realms of economics. As the largest foreign holder of U.S. treasuries, China's financial leverage over the United States has contributed to a complex power dynamic with substantial geopolitical consequences. In the event of heightened political tensions or economic conflict, the potential for China to utilize its vast holdings of U.S. debt as a tool of strategic influence cannot be overlooked. This creates a delicate balance of power, where economic decisions can have direct implications on global security and stability. The inherent interdependence in the U.S.-China relationship amplifies the significance of debt dynamics in shaping geopolitical strategies and negotiations. Moreover, the dependence of the United States on Chinese capital underscores the need for careful navigation of their financial ties, especially within the context of broader competition and cooperation on the world stage. The risk of weaponizing debt is a pressing reality, as it could precipitate a domino effect across markets and international relations, ultimately reconfiguring the geopolitical landscape. Furthermore, the potential for economic coercion through debt manipulation adds an additional layer of complexity to an already intricate relationship, necessitating a nuanced understanding of the intersection between finance and geopolitics. Ultimately, the geostrategic implications of the debt dynamics between the U.S. and China transcend traditional economic considerations, requiring policymakers and strategists to adopt a comprehensive approach that encompasses both financial and geopolitical dimensions.

Political Ramifications of Financial Interdependence

The political ramifications of the deep financial interdependence between the United States and China reverberate across the global geopolitical landscape. At the core of this intricate relationship lies a complex web of economic power dynamics and strategic influence that demand careful examination. This section delves into the nuanced confluence of politics and economics, shedding light on the multifaceted implications stemming from the intertwined fiscal interests of the two superpowers.

An inherent facet of this interdependence is the inherent leverage it yields over policy decisions and geopolitical strategies. Both nations grapple with the delicate balance of leveraging economic relations for political gain while striving to mitigate the potential risks and vulnerabilities arising from such entwined financial ties. The intricacies of trade imbalances, currency manipulation, and debt ownership contribute to an intricate dance of power negotiations and political maneuvering.

Furthermore, the political ramification extends to the realm of international diplomacy and security. As the U.S. and China navigate their financial entanglement, the intricacies of foreign policy, regional security, and global governance are significantly impacted. Their approach to shared challenges such as climate change, international development, and human rights is inevitably shaped by the specter of mutual economic dependence, leading to a complex interplay of cooperation and competition on the global stage.

Moreover, the bilateral financial ties also exert profound systemic effects on global institutions and multilateral frameworks. The World Trade Organization, International Monetary Fund, and other international regulatory bodies can become arenas for diplomatic showdowns and strategic positioning, as both nations seek to influence the rules and norms governing the global economic order. The extent to which their financial interdependence facilitates or complicates collective action on pressing global issues poses critical questions for the future trajectory of international relations.

In conclusion, the political ramifications of the deep-seated financial interdependence between the U.S. and China permeate every facet of global affairs, encompassing economics, security, diplomacy, and institutional dynamics. Understanding and navigating these complexities require a comprehensive grasp of the underlying power structures, strategic motivations, and evolving geopolitical realities in an increasingly interconnected world.

Economic Consequences of Sino-American Financial Ties

The economic consequences of Sino-American financial ties are far-reaching and multifaceted, exerting significant influence on the global economy. As two of the world's largest economies, the United States and China share an intricate web of financial interdependence that impacts various aspects of domestic and international economic dynamics. The cross-border flow of capital, goods, and services between these two powerhouse nations has not only shaped their respective economic landscapes but has also reverberated across markets worldwide. Central to this financial nexus is the complex relationship between the US dollar and the Chinese yuan, which underpins the functioning of global financial systems and profoundly affects trade balances, exchange rates, and monetary policies. The close entwinement of the US and Chinese economies has propelled both countries into a state of symbiotic coexistence, where developments in one nation can send ripples through the other. From a macroeconomic perspective, the sheer scale of bilateral trade and investment links between the US and China has altered the traditional paradigms of economic theory and practice. The emergence of China as a manufacturing hub and the primary supplier of a myriad of goods to the U.S. market has redefined the dynamics of international trade, disrupting established supply chains and reshaping global consumption patterns. Conversely, Chinese firms and sovereign entities have become pivotal creditors for the US government, holding substantial amounts of American debt securities. This accumulation of US treasury holdings by China provides a critical source of funding for the expansive US budget deficit and shapes the trajectory of US fiscal policy. Furthermore, the intricate financial entanglement between the two nations influences geopolitical strategies, adding a layer of complexity to diplomatic relations and international negotiations. As such, the economic consequences of Sino-American financial ties extend beyond mere balance sheets and profit margins, permeating into the realms of national security, technological innovation, and global governance. Understanding these repercussions is paramount in navigating the ever-evolving landscape of international finance and diplomacy, as the intertwined fates of the US and China continue to shape the contours of the global economic order.

Case Studies: Real-World Impacts of U.S. Debt

In order to comprehensively understand the significant real-world impacts of U.S. debt on its relations with China, it is crucial to delve into specific case studies that illustrate the multifaceted nature of this financial interdependence. One such case study revolves around the intricate dynamics of trade imbalances and currency manipulation, shedding light on how these factors have influenced the economic landscapes of both nations. Furthermore, the implications of U.S. debt are exemplified through the intricate web of global supply chains, where the reliance on Chinese manufacturing and U.S. consumer demand intertwine to produce a complex economic symbiosis. By exploring the real-world ramifications of U.S. debt through these case studies, we can gain valuable insights into the intricacies of the economic ties between the two global powers. Moreover, the examination of specific scenarios and their repercussions offers a nuanced understanding that transcends theoretical discussions. Through these case studies, we can discern the profound impact of U.S. debt on international trade, investment patterns, and geopolitical strategies, ultimately highlighting the significance of navigating this relationship with prudence and foresight.

Future Trajectories: Predictions and Possibilities

The complex intertwining of the U.S. and Chinese economies presents a fascinating landscape for assessing future trajectories and potential outcomes. Foremost among the many considerations is the evolving power dynamics between these two global giants, as well as how their economic interdependence will continue to shape geopolitical negotiations and strategies. The repercussions of this interdependence are far-reaching, extending beyond trade and finance to encompass broader political, military, and technological realms. As we venture into the future, several key predictions and possibilities emerge. One such prediction revolves around the continuous balancing act required by both nations as they seek to maintain economic stability while also preserving their respective strategic interests. Additionally, the potential for increased diversification of trading partners for both countries looms large on the horizon. This diversification could serve as a hedge against the risks associated with heavy reliance on any single partner. Furthermore, the realm of innovation and technology presents a ripe arena for potential collaboration and competition between the U.S. and China. The race to lead in emerging technologies, such as artificial intelligence, quantum computing, and clean energy, holds enormous consequences for global leadership and economic dominance. Crafting policies that foster healthy competition while mitigating the risks of technological decoupling will be a delicate yet crucial task for both nations. Moreover, the global response to climate change and sustainability will significantly impact the U.S.-China economic relationship. Joint efforts in green technology and sustainable development could become pivotal areas of cooperation, potentially shifting the dynamics of their interdependence. Finally, the potential for recalibration of global financial structures, including shifts in currency and investment patterns, could bring about significant changes in the U.S.-China economic interdependence. These and other factors will undoubtedly shape the future trajectories of their relationship, ultimately defining the nature of the global economic order.

Conclusion: Navigating a Complex Financial Relationship

Navigating the complex financial relationship between the United States and China demands a nuanced and multifaceted approach. As the two largest economies in the world, their interdependence is undeniable. The intricate web of financial ties, trade imbalances, and geopolitical considerations has far-reaching implications that require careful navigation. Forecasts for the future trajectory of this relationship are fraught with uncertainty, particularly as both nations seek to maintain economic strength while addressing domestic and global challenges.

One potential path forward involves reimagining the nature of economic interdependence. Both countries must strive to foster cooperation rather than competition, seeking opportunities for mutual benefit while respecting each other's economic sovereignty. This entails constructive dialogue, transparency, and a commitment to fair and reciprocal trade practices.

Moreover, managing the complex financial relationship necessitates an acute awareness of geopolitical shifts and global economic trends. As the dynamics of power evolve on the international stage, the U.S. and China must be attuned to the potential impacts on their financial ties. Anticipating and adapting to these changes will be crucial in fostering a stable and sustainable economic partnership.

In conclusion, navigating the complex financial relationship between the U.S. and China requires strategic foresight, diplomacy, and an unwavering commitment to shared prosperity. Both nations possess immense economic influence, and the manner in which they engage with one another holds significant implications for the global economy. By prioritizing collaboration and engaging in principled negotiations, the U.S. and China can chart a course towards a symbiotic economic relationship that fosters stability, growth, and resilience in the face of evolving global challenges.

INVESTMENT IN RESEARCH AND DEVELOPMENT

OVERVIEW OF R&D INVESTMENTS IN THE GLOBAL CONTEXT

R&D investments form a crucial component of the economic strategies of leading global economies. The pursuit of scientific and technological advancement has become emblematic of nations vying for competitive advantages in the modern era. Across the world, governments and private enterprises allocate substantial resources to R&D with an eye towards driving innovation and fostering growth. In particular, leading economies such as the United States, China, Japan, Germany, and South Korea have emerged as frontrunners in R&D expenditure, consistently outpacing other nations. These countries view R&D as pivotal to maintaining their position on the cutting edge of technology and securing a sustainable economic future. Furthermore, they recognize the interplay between R&D investments, productivity gains, and long-term economic prosperity. As a result, these nations have incorporated robust frameworks and incentives to incentivize R&D spending, cultivating environments conducive to groundbreaking discoveries and breakthrough innovations. This global emphasis on R&D underscores its significance as a strategic tool for enhancing competitiveness, advancing knowledge frontiers, and ensuring relevance in an increasingly interconnected and technologically driven world.

Historical Trends in U.S. Research and Development

The United States has a rich history of groundbreaking innovation and technological advancement, largely driven by significant investments in research and development (R&D). Throughout the 20th and 21st centuries, the U.S. has been at the forefront of scientific discovery, leading to transformative developments in various fields including aerospace, pharmaceuticals, information technology, and engineering. One of the earliest examples of this commitment to R&D can be traced back to the establishment of major research universities such as MIT, Stanford, and Caltech, which became hubs for pioneering scientific research and collaboration with industry. The post-World War II era marked a crucial turning point, with the U.S. government's substantial investment in scientific research culminating in the creation of institutions like the National Science Foundation (NSF) and the National Aeronautics and Space Administration (NASA). These initiatives not only propelled the country ahead in the space race but also galvanized a culture of innovation and technological progress. The 1980s and 1990s saw the rise of Silicon Valley, a hotbed for entrepreneurial activity and disruptive technological advances powered by risk-taking venture capitalists and brilliant minds from around the world. This period witnessed the birth of companies like Apple, Microsoft, and Google, shaping the trajectory of global R&D and redefining the possibilities of consumer technology. The dot-com boom and subsequent bust brought both exuberance and caution, highlighting the dynamic nature of the U.S. R&D landscape. In recent years, the U.S. has continued to lead in areas such as artificial intelligence, biotechnology, and renewable energy, leveraging its world-class research institutions, robust intellectual property protections, and a dynamic ecosystem of start-ups and established enterprises. However, amidst these successes, there are growing concerns about declining federal funding for basic research, potential talent shortages in critical STEM fields, and increasing competition from other countries investing heavily in R&D. Analyzing the historical trends in U.S. R&D unveils a complex tapestry of achievement, resilience, and the need for sustained commitment to innovation in order to retain global leadership in an increasingly competitive environment.

Evolution of Chinese Investment in Research and Development

China's investment in research and development (R&D) has undergone a remarkable evolution over the past few decades, reflecting the country's ambitious drive to transform itself into a global technological powerhouse. The early stages of China's R&D efforts were characterized by a heavy emphasis on fundamental research in fields such as agriculture, health, and energy. This initial phase laid the groundwork for the subsequent rapid expansion and diversification of R&D activities across various sectors. As China transitioned from being an agrarian society to a manufacturing-centric economy, the government strategically prioritized R&D investments to bolster innovation and competitiveness. The nation's leadership recognized the pivotal role of technology in driving sustainable economic growth and sought to harness R&D as a catalyst for development. Over time, China's R&D landscape witnessed a shift towards applied research and cutting-edge technological advancements, aligning with the country's aspirations to lead in emerging fields such as artificial intelligence, quantum computing, and biotechnology. The evolution of Chinese R&D investment is also closely tied to the nation's open-door policy, which entailed collaborations with international partners and the infusion of foreign expertise and capital. This strategic approach facilitated knowledge transfer and contributed to the rapid expansion of China's technological capabilities. Concurrently, the government introduced numerous incentive programs and favorable policies to stimulate R&D spending by domestic enterprises, fostering a vibrant ecosystem conducive to innovation. The surge in R&D investment within China has not only propelled the nation to the forefront of global technological innovation but has also catalyzed the emergence of homegrown multinational corporations, poised to compete on the world stage. Notably, the growing synergy between academia, industry, and government has bolstered China's R&D ecosystem, enabling seamless translation of cutting-edge research into commercially viable products and services. Furthermore, the intertwining of R&D with China's broader strategic initiatives, such as the Belt and Road Initiative and Made in China 2025, illustrates the intricate linkages between technological advancement and national development objectives. The evolution of Chinese R&D investment epitomizes the nation's unwavering commitment to fostering an innovation-driven economy and underscores its transformative journey from imitator to innovator, with far-reaching implications for the global technological landscape.

Comparative Analysis of R&D Expenditures

When comparing the research and development (R&D) expenditures of the United States and China, it is essential to delve into various aspects that underpin these investments. The comparative analysis involves assessing not only the sheer magnitude of R&D spending but also the allocation of resources across different sectors, the role of government policies, and the overall impact on technological innovation and economic growth. The United States has traditionally been a global leader in R&D investments, with a strong emphasis on cutting-edge technologies in sectors such as aerospace, pharmaceuticals, and information technology. In contrast, China has rapidly expanded its R&D budget over the past few decades, focusing on emerging industries like renewable energy, artificial intelligence, and biotechnology. Understanding the distribution of R&D funds across these areas provides valuable insights into the strategic priorities of each nation and their long-term vision for technological advancement. Government policies play a crucial role in shaping R&D expenditures in both countries. In the United States, tax incentives, grants, and subsidies have historically supported private sector innovation, while federal agencies such as the National Institutes of Health and the Department of Defense have been significant drivers of scientific research. On the other hand, China's centralized planning allows for targeted investments in key strategic industries, often through state-owned enterprises and research institutions. Analyzing the impact of these policies on the quantity and quality of R&D outcomes sheds light on the differing approaches to fostering innovation and driving economic development. Furthermore, a comparative analysis of R&D expenditures must consider the collaboration between public and private entities and the influence of educational institutions. In the U.S., universities and research centers have been pivotal in advancing fundamental scientific knowledge and translating it into commercial applications. China, too, has increasingly leveraged its academic resources to bolster R&D capabilities, forging partnerships with domestic and international stakeholders to enhance knowledge transfer and technology diffusion. Ultimately, the comparative analysis of R&D expenditures serves not just as a barometer of technological prowess, but also as a lens through which to examine each country's trajectory towards sustaining economic dynamism and competitiveness in the global landscape.

Government Policies Impacting R&D in the U.S. and China

Government policies play a crucial role in shaping the landscape of Research and Development (R&D) in both the United States and China. The incentives and regulations put in place by the respective governments significantly impact the direction, scale, and effectiveness of R&D activities within their borders. In the United States, the government has historically played a pivotal role in funding basic research through institutions such as the National Science Foundation (NSF), the National Institutes of Health (NIH), and the Department of Defense (DoD). Additionally, tax incentives and grants have been instrumental in encouraging private sector investment in R&D, leading to breakthrough innovations across various industries. The U.S. government's focus on fostering a conducive environment for innovation has contributed to its status as a global leader in cutting-edge technologies and scientific discoveries. However, concerns have been raised about the decline in federal funding for R&D as a percentage of GDP over the years, potentially impacting America's long-term competitiveness and technological prowess. On the other hand, China has adopted a strategic approach to R&D investment, with a clear emphasis on prioritizing key areas such as artificial intelligence, biotechnology, and information technology. The Chinese government has established ambitious R&D targets and allocated substantial resources to achieve these goals, including through initiatives like the Made in China 2025 strategy. Moreover, policies promoting collaboration between academia, industry, and government have driven significant advancements in R&D capabilities within China. Through measures like tax incentives, funding grants, and intellectual property protection, China aims to incentivize domestic and foreign entities to conduct R&D activities within its borders. However, concerns persist regarding issues such as intellectual property rights enforcement and transparency in the allocation of research funds. Additionally, geopolitical tensions have led to scrutiny of China's R&D practices, further influencing global perceptions of its innovation ecosystem. The divergent approaches of the U.S. and China in structuring their R&D policies reflect not only their distinct political and economic systems but also signal the competitive dynamics at play in the global innovation arena. As both nations navigate challenges related to funding, regulatory frameworks, and international collaboration, their R&D policies will continue to shape the future trajectory of technological progress and economic leadership on the world stage.

Role of Private Sector Innovation

Private sector innovation plays a pivotal role in driving research and development (R&D) efforts, particularly in the context of the United States and China. The influence of private enterprises in shaping technological advancements, driving economic growth, and enhancing global competitiveness cannot be overstated. In the U.S., tech giants such as Google, Apple, Microsoft, and countless startups have been at the forefront of transformative innovations, spanning from consumer electronics to cutting-edge software solutions. This has not only propelled the U.S. economy but also fostered an ecosystem conducive to pioneering R&D initiatives. Similarly, in China, the rise of influential companies like Huawei, Alibaba, Tencent, and numerous rapidly emerging firms reflect the significant impact of private sector innovation on China's R&D landscape.

Private enterprises are often agile and have the resources to take substantial risks, investing in long-term projects that may not align with short-term profit objectives. This approach fosters groundbreaking discoveries and technological breakthroughs that redefine industries and drive progress. Moreover, private sector entities are adept at commercializing R&D outcomes, translating scientific advancements into tangible products and services that benefit society at large. Through strategic investments and partnerships, these companies collaborate with research institutions and academia to leverage diverse expertise and resources, thereby amplifying the impact of R&D efforts.

However, while private sector innovation brings about unique advantages, it also poses challenges. Issues of intellectual property rights, market monopolization, and ethical considerations in emerging technologies necessitate robust governance frameworks. Moreover, the unequal distribution of R&D investments across sectors and regions underscores the need for inclusive and balanced innovation policies. In this regard, governments play a crucial role in regulating and incentivizing private sector R&D, fostering an environment where innovation flourishes while addressing societal concerns.

As we delve deeper into the intricate interplay between private sector innovation and R&D, it becomes apparent that the synergy between industry, academia, and government is essential for sustainable progress. By understanding the multifaceted dynamics at play, we can harness the full potential of private sector innovation to drive inclusive growth, address global challenges, and propel both the U.S. and China towards a future defined by technological prowess and socioeconomic prosperity.

Influence of Educational Institutions on National R&D Capabilities

Educational institutions play a pivotal role in shaping national research and development (R&D) capabilities. With an emphasis on fostering innovation, these institutions serve as the breeding ground for future scientists, engineers, and researchers who will drive R&D efforts. The synergy between academia and industry is crucial in leveraging the potential of educational institutions to contribute to the nation's R&D landscape. Through collaborative initiatives, such as joint research programs or industry-sponsored projects, universities and research institutions can channel their expertise and intellectual resources towards addressing real-world challenges and advancing technological frontiers.

Furthermore, educational institutions act as catalysts for knowledge transfer and dissemination. By nurturing a culture of curiosity and intellectual exploration, these establishments equip students with the critical thinking and problem-solving skills essential for driving R&D progress. Research-oriented universities often lead cutting-edge investigations in various fields, thereby enriching the reservoir of scientific knowledge and technological breakthroughs. Additionally, incubators and technology transfer offices within academic settings facilitate the transition of innovative ideas and discoveries from the laboratory to commercial applications, propelling the nation's economic growth.

Moreover, the collaborative networks formed by educational institutions provide a fertile ground for interdisciplinary research and cross-sector partnerships. Such collaboration fosters a dynamic exchange of ideas and perspectives, amplifying the scope and impact of R&D endeavors. These interactions not only bolster the depth of expertise but also cultivate a diverse pool of talent necessary for sustained R&D advancement. As a result, educational institutions act as engines of innovation, driving the transformation of theoretical concepts into practical solutions that address societal needs and fuel economic progress.

The influence of educational institutions on national R&D capabilities extends beyond the borders, contributing to global knowledge dissemination and fostering international collaborations. By attracting top-tier faculty and students from around the world, these institutions harness a diverse spectrum of insights and talents, further enriching R&D environments. Additionally, through joint international research initiatives and knowledge-sharing agreements, educational institutions actively contribute to advancing global R&D frontiers, transcending geographical constraints in the pursuit of scientific excellence.

In conclusion, the influence of educational institutions on national R&D capabilities is indisputable. Their pivotal role in cultivating a culture of innovation, knowledge creation, and interdisciplinary collaboration empowers nations to continually advance the frontiers of research and development. Moreover, their contributions extend globally, amplifying the impact of R&D initiatives and fostering a vibrant ecosystem of scientific progress.

Long-term Outcomes of R&D on Economic Growth

Research and development (R&D) activities have long been recognized as crucial drivers of economic growth and technological advancement. A sustained commitment to R&D can yield far-reaching impacts on a nation's economy, innovation capacity, and global competitiveness over the long term. This section delves into the multi-faceted outcomes of R&D investments on economic growth, elucidating the transformative effects that reverberate across industries and national boundaries.

One of the primary outcomes of robust R&D investment is the proliferation of new technologies and innovations, which can revolutionize industrial processes, enhance productivity, and catalyze the emergence of entirely new sectors. These technological advancements, stemming from R&D endeavors, often lead to increased efficiency, reduced costs, and the creation of high-value jobs, thereby bolstering overall economic growth. Furthermore, R&D initiatives foster a culture of creativity and problem-solving, laying the groundwork for sustainable economic progress and resilience in the face of global challenges.

Moreover, R&D not only drives economic growth but also acts as a catalyst for spurring further investment and attracting human capital and foreign direct investment. Nations with a strong R&D ecosystem tend to attract top talent and international partnerships, leading to knowledge transfer, cross-border collaboration, and the establishment of vibrant innovation clusters. Such dynamic ecosystems breed an environment conducive to entrepreneurship and the formation of startup enterprises, which contribute significantly to employment generation and economic dynamism.

In addition, the long-term outcomes of R&D extend beyond economic metrics, influencing societal well-being and quality of life. Breakthroughs in healthcare, renewable energy, environmental sustainability, and other critical domains are often the direct result of sustained R&D investments. From life-saving medical treatments to clean technologies, R&D plays an instrumental role in addressing complex social challenges and improving overall welfare, thus underscoring its profound and wide-ranging impact on economic and human development.

Beyond domestic spheres, R&D investments also underpin a nation's ability to assert itself as a global leader in innovation and technology. By nurturing a vibrant R&D landscape, nations position themselves at the forefront of the knowledge economy, leading to the development of globally sought-after products and services. This not only enhances a country's trade balance but also solidifies its strategic relevance and influence on the international stage, fostering diplomatic and economic relations.

In conclusion, the long-term outcomes of R&D on economic growth are multifaceted, encompassing technological breakthroughs, enhanced competitiveness, societal advancement, and global leadership. Recognizing the enduring impact of R&D endeavors, nations can strategically chart their path towards sustainable and inclusive economic prosperity, innovation-driven development, and preeminence in the global arena.

Implications for Global Competitiveness and Technological Leadership

The implications of research and development (R&D) activities in the United States and China extend far beyond their national borders, significantly impacting global competitiveness and technological leadership. As both countries invest heavily in R&D, the outcomes have the potential to reshape the international economic and technological landscape. In terms of global competitiveness, the level of R&D investment directly correlates with a nation's ability to innovate and develop cutting-edge technologies. A robust R&D infrastructure fosters an environment conducive to creating high-value products and services, thereby enhancing a country's competitive edge in the global marketplace. The continued advancement of R&D capabilities in the U.S. and China amplifies their prominence as drivers of innovation and economic influence on the world stage. Moreover, technological leadership is closely intertwined with R&D investments, as it fuels advancements that propel nations to the forefront of various industries and sectors. By spearheading breakthroughs in areas such as artificial intelligence, biotechnology, and renewable energy, the U.S. and China are vying for dominance in shaping the future of technology and setting industry standards. As they compete for technological supremacy, the repercussions of their progress or stagnation reverberate throughout the global economy, determining which nation leads the way in defining the technological landscape. Furthermore, the implications of global competitiveness and technological leadership extend beyond economic advantages, encompassing geopolitical influence and strategic positioning in emerging fields. The race for dominance in R&D and technological innovation has far-reaching implications for international collaboration, trade dynamics, and geopolitical alignments. As the U.S. and China drive advances in critical technologies, other nations are compelled to recalibrate their strategies to remain relevant in the ever-evolving global ecosystem. The intertwined relationship between R&D investments, global competitiveness, and technological leadership underscores the pivotal role these two superpowers play in shaping the trajectory of the global economy and technological development. To fully comprehend the implications of their endeavors in R&D, further analysis is imperative to gauge the overarching impact on international relations, global trade patterns, and the balance of power in the realm of innovation and technology.

Future Projections: Trends and Possibilities in U.S. and Chinese R&D

As we look toward the future, it is essential to examine the potential trajectories of research and development (R&D) in both the United States and China. The role of R&D in shaping the global economic landscape cannot be overstated, and the choices made by these two influential nations will undoubtedly have far-reaching implications. One of the key trends that is expected to continue shaping R&D in the U.S. is the increasing emphasis on interdisciplinary collaboration. With complex challenges requiring multifaceted solutions, the integration of diverse fields such as technology, healthcare, and environmental sustainability will become paramount. Additionally, the U.S. is likely to witness a surge in public-private partnerships aimed at driving innovation across various sectors. In contrast, China's R&D landscape is anticipated to further expand and diversify, with the country investing heavily in frontier technologies such as artificial intelligence, quantum computing, and biotechnology. The strategic focus on bolstering core technological capabilities aligns with China's ambition to lead the global innovation race. Moreover, the integration of R&D into the Belt and Road Initiative underscores China's commitment to leveraging research and development for geopolitical influence and economic expansion. Looking ahead, the trajectory of U.S. R&D will also be shaped by policy interventions and funding decisions, particularly in response to global challenges such as climate change and pandemics. Concurrently, China's R&D landscape will continue to evolve under the framework of its national innovation-driven development strategy, with a strong emphasis on indigenous innovation and international collaboration. The possibilities for synergy and competition between the U.S. and China in the realm of research and development are vast. Collaborative endeavors in areas of mutual interest, such as sustainable energy solutions and space exploration, could redefine the global innovation ecosystem. Conversely, intensifying competition in emerging fields might fuel technological rivalry with profound geopolitical implications. Anticipating these dynamics requires a nuanced understanding of the intricate interplay between scientific advancement, economic dynamism, and geopolitical leverage. Together, the trajectories of U.S. and Chinese R&D will profoundly impact the future of global technological leadership, economic strength, and societal well-being.

THE RISE OF BRICS

INTRODUCTION TO BRICS: AN EMERGING POWER BLOC

The concept of BRICS represents an amalgamation of the world's most influential emerging economies – Brazil, Russia, India, China, and South Africa. Their collective significance in the global economy is indisputable, as their combined GDP accounts for around a quarter of the world's economic output. The emergence of BRICS has shifted the traditional power dynamics and economic landscape, challenging the previously established dominance of Western economies. With substantial natural resources, burgeoning markets, and growing populations, these nations have become pivotal players in shaping the future trajectory of international trade, finance, and geopolitics. As a result, policymakers, investors, and analysts closely monitor the economic performance and strategic decisions of BRICS countries, recognizing their potential to significantly impact global economic trends and governance.

Historical Overview of BRICS Formation

The emergence of BRICS as a geopolitical bloc is rooted in the dynamic global shifts that began to unfold in the early 21st century. The term 'BRICS' was initially coined by economist Jim O'Neill in 2001, as he foresaw an impending shift in the global economic landscape. This visionary concept encompassed the collective potential of five major emerging economies: Brazil, Russia, India, China, and later South Africa, solidifying their position as significant players on the world stage. The formation of BRICS marked a paradigmatic shift in the international relations framework, transitioning from uni-polar dominance to a multi-polar world order. It signified the assertion of emerging economies, primarily representing diverse cultural, historical, and political backgrounds, in the pursuit of mutual development, cooperation, and influence. As a testament to its significance, the inaugural BRIC summit was convened in 2009, symbolizing an unprecedented step toward forging strategic partnerships and fostering collaboration among the member countries. The historical underpinnings of BRICS trace back to the shared aspirations for economic development, social upliftment, and global influence, thus transcending conventional power dynamics and paving the way for a transformed global socioeconomic narrative.

Economic Indicators: Analyzing GDP Growth

Gross Domestic Product (GDP) serves as a fundamental measure of economic performance and prosperity for nations within the BRICS alliance. In this section, we delve into a comprehensive analysis of the GDP growth dynamics across Brazil, Russia, India, China, and South Africa. Understanding the trajectory of each nation's GDP growth provides valuable insights into their economic development, potential challenges, and implications for global economic structures.

Brazil, as a key player in the BRICS coalition, has showcased varying GDP growth rates over the past decade. Factors such as political instability, fluctuating commodity prices, and structural impediments have contributed to Brazil's economic performance. Through a meticulous examination of its GDP growth patterns, we aim to uncover the nuanced factors influencing Brazil's economic landscape and trajectory within the BRICS framework.

Russia's GDP growth dynamics are intrinsically linked to its energy sector and geopolitical developments. This section draws attention to the impact of oil prices, international sanctions, and domestic policies on Russia's economic indicators. By dissecting the nuances of Russia's GDP growth, we aim to provide a holistic view of its economic progress and resilience amidst external pressures.

India, renowned for its burgeoning service sector and demographic dividend, presents a compelling case for analyzing GDP growth patterns. We explore the impact of domestic reforms, technological advancements, and global market integration on India's economic indicators. Our analysis seeks to unravel the drivers propelling India's GDP growth and the challenges that warrant strategic attention from policymakers and global stakeholders.

China's remarkable ascent as a global economic powerhouse has been underscored by its sustained GDP growth over several decades. This segment delves into the intricacies of China's economic model, the role of state-driven initiatives, and the challenges accompanying its transition towards innovation-led growth. By scrutinizing China's GDP growth trajectory, we aim to distill valuable insights into the sustainability of its economic momentum and the evolving global impact of its economic policies.

South Africa's GDP growth narrative illuminates the influence of socioeconomic disparities, structural reforms, and global market volatilities. This section critically analyzes South Africa's economic journey within the BRICS paradigm, shedding light on the intricate interplay of domestic policies, external trade dynamics, and developmental imperatives shaping its GDP growth trajectory.

The holistic examination of GDP growth across the BRICS nations unveils the complex interconnections between internal economic policies, global market forces, and socio-political dynamics shaping their development trajectories. By juxtaposing these analyses, we can glean valuable insights into the collective and individual prospects of BRICS economies, thereby facilitating informed discussions and strategic foresight in navigating the evolving global economic landscape.

BRICS vs. G7: Comparative Economic Development

The comparison between the BRICS nations and the G7 countries provides an insightful perspective into the global economic landscape. The G7, consisting of the United States, Japan, Germany, United Kingdom, France, Canada, and Italy, has traditionally held significant influence in shaping global economic policies. On the other hand, the emergence of BRICS comprising Brazil, Russia, India, China, and South Africa has introduced a new dynamic to the international economic order.

One of the key contrasts between BRICS and G7 lies in their GDP growth rates. While the G7 economies have exhibited slower GDP growth in recent years, the BRICS nations have experienced more rapid expansion. This trend underscores the shifting balance of economic power from traditional Western powers towards rising economies in the East and the Global South. Moreover, the

BRICS countries collectively account for a substantial portion of the world's population, adding further weight to their economic influence.

An important aspect of comparative evaluation is the performance of key sectors in both blocs. The G7 economies have historically been dominant in sectors such as finance, technology, and advanced manufacturing. In contrast, the BRICS nations have excelled in sectors such as energy, natural resources, and infrastructure development. This divergence in sectoral strengths has contributed to varying patterns of trade and investment between the two groups.

Furthermore, examining the demographics of the BRICS and G7 nations reveals distinct population dynamics. The G7 nations generally have aging populations, leading to challenges related to labor force participation and healthcare expenditures. Conversely, the BRICS countries possess youthful populations, presenting opportunities for rapid workforce expansion and consumer markets. These demographic disparities have significant implications for future economic growth and societal development within each bloc.

It is also crucial to consider the role of international institutions and global governance structures in this comparative analysis. The G7 nations have historically maintained significant influence in organizations such as the IMF, World Bank, and WTO, shaping global economic policies and regulations. However, the collective clout of the BRICS nations has led to calls for reforming these institutions to better reflect the evolving economic realities of the 21st century.

In conclusion, the comparative assessment of BRICS and G7 economies underscores the transformative shifts occurring in the global economic order. The rise of BRICS signals a rebalancing of economic power and influence, challenging established norms and reshaping the contours of international trade, investment, and governance.

Sector-Wise Growth Analysis in BRICS Nations

The BRICS nations, comprising Brazil, Russia, India, China, and South Africa, have collectively emerged as a significant economic force on the global stage. As we delve into the sector-wise growth analysis of these nations, it becomes apparent that each country has made distinct advancements within specific industries, contributing to the overall economic prowess of the BRICS bloc. Beginning with China, it is evident that the manufacturing sector has been a cornerstone of its economic development, fueling its export-driven growth. The rapid expansion of China's manufacturing industry has not only propelled its domestic economic growth but has also positioned the nation as a global manufacturing hub. Furthermore, India has exhibited remarkable growth in its information technology and services sector, leveraging its skilled workforce to become a prominent player in the global IT outsourcing market. The burgeoning software services and business process outsourcing industries have significantly contributed to India's economic output and employment generation. Moving to Brazil, the agricultural sector has traditionally played a pivotal role in its economy, with extensive arable land and abundant natural resources supporting agricultural production and export. Additionally, Brazil has experienced substantial growth in its renewable energy sector, particularly in ethanol and biofuel production, fostering sustainability and environmental consciousness. Russia, renowned for its vast reserves of natural resources, has seen significant growth in its energy sector, particularly in oil and gas exploration and export. The hydrocarbon industry has been pivotal in driving Russia's economic expansion and geopolitical influence. Lastly, South Africa has demonstrated robust growth in its mining and minerals sector, harnessing its rich mineral deposits to drive export revenues and industrial growth. With a focus on platinum, gold, and diamonds, South Africa has cemented its position as a key player in the global mining industry. Through this comprehensive sector-wise analysis, it is evident that the BRICS nations have diversified their economies across various sectors, capitalizing on their unique strengths and resources to foster sustainable economic growth and global competitiveness.

Influence of Research and Development Investments

Research and development (R&D) investments play a pivotal role in shaping the economic trajectory of the BRICS nations. These investments are instrumental in fostering innovation, driving technological advancements, and enhancing the overall competitiveness of these emerging economies. As each nation seeks to solidify its position in the global market, strategic allocation of resources towards R&D becomes increasingly critical. China, for instance, has significantly increased its R&D spending in recent years, propelling the country into a leading position in various technological domains. India, too, has demonstrated a commitment to bolstering its R&D capabilities, particularly in the realms of pharmaceuticals, IT, and renewable energy. Similarly, Russia has placed emphasis on leveraging R&D to diversify its economy beyond natural resources, with a focus on aerospace, nuclear technology, and advanced materials. Brazil and South Africa have also recognized the indispensable nature of R&D in driving sustainable growth and maintaining a competitive edge in the global arena. These investments not only fuel innovation but also contribute to job creation, skill development, and knowledge dissemination within the respective economies. Moreover, by fostering a conducive environment for R&D, the BRICS nations can attract top talent, both domestically and internationally, thereby strengthening their intellectual capital. The increasing collaboration and joint R&D initiatives among BRICS countries further underscore the significance of these investments. By sharing expertise and resources, the member nations can collectively surmount challenges, accelerate progress, and emerge as formidable players in the global innovation landscape. However, it is imperative to address challenges such as intellectual property rights, bureaucratic hurdles, and funding constraints to fully realize the potential of R&D investments. Effective policies, collaborative frameworks, and sustained commitment from both public and private sectors will be essential in harnessing the transformative power of research and development across the BRICS economies.

Trade Dynamics within BRICS

Trade dynamics within BRICS, comprising Brazil, Russia, India, China, and South Africa, reflect a complex interplay of factors that have significant implications for global commerce. The combined economic might of these nations has reshaped the landscape of international trade, engendering a new era of multipolarity. A nuanced understanding of the trade dynamics within BRICS necessitates an examination of various facets, including bilateral and multilateral trade agreements, sector-specific trade patterns, and the impact on global supply chains. Inter-regional trade initiatives among BRICS members have not only bolstered their individual economic clout but have also fostered extensive strategic partnerships. China's position as the leading trading partner for many BRICS countries underscores its pivotal role in shaping trade dynamics within the bloc. Additionally, India's and

Brazil's efforts to diversify their trade relations within the group have yielded mixed results, presenting a compelling tableau of evolving trade strategies.

Challenges Facing BRICS Economies

The BRICS bloc, comprising Brazil, Russia, India, China, and South Africa, has undeniably emerged as a formidable force in the global economy. However, amidst their swift rise, these economies are not immune to challenges that warrant comprehensive analysis. One of the primary challenges facing BRICS economies is the issue of structural reforms. Each member nation faces the arduous task of advancing structural reforms to sustain growth and development. The diversity within BRICS necessitates tailored policy approaches to address issues related to infrastructure, finance, and governance. Additionally, these nations must navigate diverse political landscapes and societal structures, further complicating the reform process. Another crucial challenge is the need to address income inequality and social disparities. While economic growth has brought prosperity to many, it has also led to growing inequality within BRICS nations, presenting a pressing socio-economic challenge. Implementing inclusive policies aimed at reducing income inequality and enhancing access to education, healthcare, and social security is paramount to ensuring sustainable growth and stability. Furthermore, BRICS countries face the challenge of managing environmental sustainability amid rapid development. Balancing the pursuit of economic progress with environmental conservation demands innovative solutions and concerted efforts. Striking a harmonious equilibrium between industrial expansion and ecological preservation is pivotal for the long-term prosperity of the BRICS economies. In the realm of international relations, BRICS nations encounter the challenge of harmonizing geopolitical interests and perspectives. As these emerging powers assert their influence on the global stage, the convergence and divergence of strategic goals and foreign policies pose intricate challenges. Navigating complex geopolitical dynamics while upholding cooperative frameworks represents a delicate balance crucial for the collective advancement of BRICS. Additionally, technological advancements and digital transformations present both opportunities and challenges for BRICS economies. Embracing technological innovation while mitigating potential disruptions to traditional sectors demands astute policy measures and adaptive strategies. Harnessing the potential of digitalization to foster inclusive growth and economic diversification is imperative for the sustained relevance of BRICS nations in the global landscape. Addressing these multifaceted challenges requires proactive collaboration, astute policy frameworks, and unwavering determination. By surmounting these hurdles, BRICS economies can consolidate their position as influential global players and spearhead transformative developments that resonate across continents.

Future Trajectories: Predictions and Economic Models

As we look to envisage the future trajectories of the BRICS economies, it becomes increasingly apparent that these nations are poised to play a significant role in shaping the global economic landscape. When analyzing predictions and economic models, it is important to consider the dynamic nature of these emerging markets and the potential catalysts for their sustained growth. One key prediction is that the collective GDP of BRICS nations will continue to outpace the traditional economic powerhouses, potentially leading to a reconfiguration of global economic leadership. This realignment may also be influenced by the evolving economic models adopted by BRICS countries, each of which presents its own set of opportunities and challenges. Economic models such as China's state-led capitalism, India's burgeoning service sector, and Brazil's resource-driven growth, offer distinctive insights into the diverse paths these nations may traverse. Furthermore, predictions indicate that investment in research and development will catalyze innovation and productivity gains, further bolstering the competitiveness of these economies on the global stage. However, inherent challenges such as income inequality, institutional reforms, and geopolitical uncertainties must also be factored into these models. In specifying the trajectory of BRICS nations, it is imperative to recognize the paradigm shift in global trade dynamics. Increasing intra-BRICS trade and strategic partnerships signify a recalibration of economic interdependencies, offering profound implications for regional and global economic governance. The confluence of these factors illuminates a compelling outlook for the future of BRICS economies. As we peer into the crystal ball of economic prognostication, it is evident that foresight must be underscored by adaptability, resilience, and policy acumen. The realization of these predictions relies not only on economic prudence but also on political will and diplomatic tact. The ability of BRICS nations to navigate through the complexities of global economics and emerge as stalwarts of sustainable growth will undoubtedly reshape the contours of the global economic order.

Summary and Transition to Political Implications

In summary, the future trajectories of the BRICS countries exhibit a dynamic landscape characterized by promising opportunities while also facing significant challenges. The economic models adopted by these nations suggest a sustained growth pattern, with concerted efforts towards technological innovation and infrastructure development. However, certain impediments, including income inequality, political instability, and environmental concerns, pose formidable obstacles to their advancement. Consequently, as we transition towards an analysis of the political implications accompanying this economic ascendancy, it becomes crucial to recognize the inherent interconnectedness between economic and geopolitical dynamics.

The rise of BRICS has not only altered the global economic landscape but has also engendered a shift in power dynamics at the political level. As these nations amass greater economic influence, their political weight on the international stage becomes increasingly pronounced. This phenomenon implicates a reconfiguration of alliances, negotiations, and policy formulations, wherein the traditional stronghold of western powers is now met with a formidable challenger. Additionally, the coalescence of the BRICS nations signifies a collective voice that demands recognition and representation in various global governance forums.

Furthermore, the increasing economic prowess of BRICS presents a duality of opportunities and challenges for the incumbent global political order. While it offers prospects for enhanced collaboration, trade partnerships, and economic synergies, it also introduces complexities in navigating competing interests, divergent ideologies, and instances of geopolitical friction. It is essential to address and navigate these nuanced interplays, as they have far-reaching implications for global stability, peace, and the shaping of future geopolitical strategies.

Moreover, the rise of BRICS predicates a recalibration of power distribution within international organizations and multilateral institutions. This brings forth discussions around reforms within bodies such as the United Nations Security Council, International Monetary Fund, and World Bank, aiming to reflect the changing global economic landscape more accurately. As such, the transition towards political ramifications requires a comprehensive understanding of the evolving dynamics and the potential confluence of divergent agendas and ideologies.

In conclusion, the economic ascendancy portrayed by the BRICS bloc converges with an intricate web of political ramifications, signaling a paradigm shift in global governance structures. Understanding and addressing the cross-cutting themes of mutual cooperation, strategic competition, and collective representation remains imperative for navigating the evolving complexities embedded within the emerging global order.

POLITICAL AND ECONOMIC IMPLICATIONS OF BRICS' RISE

INTRODUCTION TO BRICS AND GLOBAL ECONOMICS

BRICS refers to an association of five major emerging economies - Brazil, Russia, India, China, and South Africa. These countries, spanning four continents, represent a significant bloc in the global economic landscape. Their combined nominal GDP accounts for nearly one-quarter of the world's economic output, underlining the substantial economic weight they collectively carry. More impressively, the BRICS nations represent about 42% of the world's population, signifying their massive consumer base and labor force. The economic significance of BRICS extends beyond their sheer size; it lies in their potential to shape the future of global economics. Each member brings unique attributes to the table. For instance, China is known for its manufacturing prowess and infrastructure development, making it a crucial player in global supply chains. India, with its thriving services sector and demographic dividend, holds the promise of becoming a powerhouse of skilled labor and innovation. Meanwhile, Russia possesses abundant natural resources, contributing significantly to the global energy market. Brazil stands out with its vibrant agricultural sector and burgeoning middle class, while South Africa serves as a gateway to African markets and is rich in minerals and commodities. Together, these nations create a diverse and complementary economic structure that wields immense clout in the international arena.

Overview of BRICS Nations' Economic Trajectories

The economic trajectories of the BRICS nations, comprising Brazil, Russia, India, China, and South Africa, have presented a compelling narrative of transformation and growth in recent decades. Each member country has experienced unique economic patterns, driven by diverse geopolitical factors, domestic policies, and global market dynamics. Brazil, as one of the early emerging economies, has shown substantial advancements in sectors such as agribusiness, energy, and technology. Russia, leveraging its vast reserves of natural resources, has undergone periods of rapid expansion and challenges influenced by fluctuations in commodity prices and geopolitical tensions. India, with its burgeoning population and expanding middle class, has exhibited remarkable resilience amid structural reforms, fostering significant developments in IT services, pharmaceuticals, and renewable energy. China's monumental rise as an economic powerhouse is characterized by unprecedented infrastructure development, industrialization, and technological innovation, propelling the nation into a position of global prominence. South Africa, as the smallest economy within the group, has grappled with issues of inequality and unemployment while also showcasing noteworthy achievements in industries such as mining, agriculture, and tourism. The trajectories of these nations underscore the varied pathways to economic development, shedding light on the complexities and nuances inherent in their respective journeys. Furthermore, the convergence of these trajectories within the BRICS framework has facilitated mutual learning, collaboration, and concerted efforts towards shaping a new paradigm in the global economic landscape. As intertwined narratives of growth and reform continue to unfold, the world keenly observes the impact of these dynamic trajectories on regional and international trade, investment patterns, and strategic partnerships, underscoring the evolving role of the BRICS bloc in the formulation of a multipolar economic order.

BRICS' Role in Shaping Global Economic Governance

The collective rise of BRICS - Brazil, Russia, India, China, and South Africa - has led to significant shifts in the landscape of global economic governance. As these nations experience rapid economic growth and development, their impact on the global economy cannot be ignored. The emergence of BRICS as a formidable entity has not only altered the dynamics of international trade and finance but has also raised fundamental questions about the existing structures of global economic governance. BRICS member countries have progressively sought greater representation and influence in international economic institutions such as the International Monetary Fund (IMF) and the World Bank. Their demands for reforms reflect a growing dissatisfaction with the prevailing power dynamics that often favor established Western economies at the expense of emerging ones. This transformative journey has compelled BRICS to reassess traditional notions of global economic governance, advocating for a more inclusive and collaborative approach that reflects the current economic realities. The establishment of the New Development Bank by BRICS demonstrates their commitment to creating alternative financial institutions that can challenge the dominance of traditional lenders. By promoting initiatives such as the Contingent Reserve Arrangement, BRICS seeks to lessen the vulnerabilities of developing economies to external financial shocks and enhance financial stability across the member nations. Furthermore, the collective influence of BRICS in international forums has enabled them to articulate viewpoints that challenge conventional economic policies and promote reforms that better align with the interests of developing nations. For instance, the bloc has consistently voiced concerns about the need for fairer global trade practices that provide equal opportunities for all participants. Their efforts have underscored the imperative of addressing issues such as trade protectionism and tariff barriers, thereby reshaping the discourse on international trade policies. In doing so, BRICS has become a champion for fostering greater equity and inclusivity in global economic governance, emphasizing the necessity of establishing a more balanced and representative framework that caters to the needs of diverse economies. As BRICS continues to assert its role in shaping global economic governance, it is evident that the collective voice of these nations will increasingly influence the direction of international economic policies, ultimately presenting new avenues for cooperation and shared prosperity.

Influence on International Trade Policies

As the BRICS nations continue to solidify their positions in the global economy, their collective influence on international trade policies has become increasingly pronounced. With their significant share of global trade and production, the BRICS bloc has been instrumental in shaping the dynamics of international trade. Their concerted efforts have had a significant impact on trade negotiations, tariff structures, and trade agreements, thereby reshaping the traditional patterns of global commerce. The combined economic clout of Brazil, Russia, India, China, and South Africa has led to a reevaluation of trade regulations and norms. In recent years, the BRICS countries have advocated for fairer and more equitable trade practices, challenging the dominance of established economic powers and calling for reforms in existing trade frameworks. This positioning has often resulted in friction with traditional trade powerhouses; nevertheless, the BRICS nations persist in their pursuit of a more balanced, inclusive, and mutually beneficial global trade landscape. Furthermore, the rise of intra-BRICS trade and economic cooperation has led to the creation of new trade networks, reducing the dependency on established markets and fostering greater regional integration among the member states. As a result, international trade policies are being reshaped by the growing clout of BRICS, which is setting a new precedent for collaborative trade initiatives and partnerships. Consequently, the adherence to multilateral trade principles is evolving as a result of the strategic alliances formed within the BRICS framework, ushering in a new era of diversity and inclusivity in global trade relations. The burgeoning impact of BRICS on international trade policies has not only opened up opportunities for their own economies but has also contributed to a paradigm shift in the broader global economic landscape.

Strategic Alliances: Formation and Evolution

Strategic alliances among the BRICS nations have played a pivotal role in shaping the global economic landscape. These alliances, forged on the basis of mutual interests and shared economic goals, have contributed significantly to the rise of the BRICS bloc as a formidable force in the international arena. The formation and evolution of these strategic alliances have not only fostered cooperation and coordination among the member countries but have also presented a paradigm shift in the traditional dynamics of global economic relations.

The formation of these strategic alliances can be traced back to the early 2000s when the BRICS nations recognized the potential for collective growth and influence in the global economy. The evolving geopolitical and economic realities prompted these countries to seek closer collaboration to amplify their voice and impact on the international stage.

Moreover, the evolution of these alliances has been characterized by a gradual transition from purely economic cooperation to broader strategic partnerships encompassing various facets of governance, security, and development. This transition reflects the maturation of the BRICS alliance, which has transcended its initial economic objectives to assume a more comprehensive and assertive role in global affairs.

Furthermore, the formation and evolution of these strategic alliances have not been devoid of challenges and complexities. The divergent domestic priorities of member nations, disparities in resource endowments, and varying levels of economic development have necessitated astute diplomatic negotiations and consensus-building processes to forge and sustain these alliances. Overcoming these challenges has been instrumental in strengthening the cohesion and resilience of the BRICS bloc.

Additionally, the ongoing evolution of these strategic alliances has engendered a recalibration of power dynamics within the global economic order. The collective influence wielded by the BRICS nations via these alliances has posed a formidable challenge to the traditional dominance exercised by Western powers in shaping and dictating global economic policies and frameworks. This shift has led to a reconfiguration of the traditional North-South discourse, thereby fostering a more equitable and inclusive approach to global economic governance.

In conclusion, the strategic alliances formed and evolved within the BRICS framework signify a watershed moment in the trajectory of global economic relations. These alliances have not only facilitated concerted action and unified positions on critical economic issues but have also heralded a new era of equilibrium in the global economic landscape. The ongoing evolution of these alliances is poised to redefine the contours of global economic governance and contribute to a more multipolar and collaborative world order.

Impact of Alliances on Western Dominance

The strategic alliances formed among the BRICS nations have had far-reaching implications for the established dominance of Western powers in global economic affairs. As these emerging economies solidify their unity and leverage their collective strength, the balance of power in the international arena is undergoing a significant shift. Firstly, the combined economic clout of Brazil, Russia, India, China, and South Africa has challenged the traditional economic supremacy of Western nations. With a growing share of global GDP and trade, the BRICS alliance upends the status quo, prompting the West to reconsider its approach to global economic governance. Moreover, the mutual support and collaboration within BRICS have resulted in concerted efforts to reform existing international institutions such as the IMF and World Bank, aiming to diminish Western control and enhance the representation of emerging economies. This has sparked debates and negotiations that hold the potential to reshape the rules and norms governing the global economic landscape. Additionally, the coalescence of BRICS countries has fostered the development of alternative financial mechanisms and institutions, reducing reliance on Western-dominated systems such as the US dollar as the global reserve currency. The establishment of institutions like the New Development Bank and Contingent Reserve Arrangement not only strengthens the financial autonomy of BRICS members but also offers alternative sources of funding and assistance to developing nations, challenging the historical dynamics of dependency on Western aid and influence. Furthermore, BRICS' joint efforts in forging trade partnerships with other regions and nations have contributed to diversifying economic linkages outside the Western sphere of influence. By cultivating new trade routes and investment channels, BRICS members are chipping away at the long-established Western economic hegemony and promoting more equitable and mutually beneficial global economic interactions. In essence, the impact of BRICS alliances on Western dominance transcends mere economic competition, signaling a profound reconfiguration of power structures and norms in the international economic order.

Analysis of BRICS' Unified Negotiation Strategies

BRICS, representing five major emerging economies—Brazil, Russia, India, China, and South Africa—has significantly enhanced its collective influence in the global economic landscape through strategic negotiation strategies. This section delves into an in-depth analysis of the unified negotiation tactics employed by BRICS to shape international trade policies and reshape the established global economic order.

One of the key elements underpinning BRICS' negotiation strength is their collective bargaining power, stemming from their combined economic weight and potential market influence. By leveraging their vast consumer base and natural resources, BRICS members have effectively pursued joint negotiation positions on multilateral trade agreements, financial governance, and development assistance that challenge the historically dominant role of Western nations.

Furthermore, BRICS' unique approach to negotiations is characterized by a focus on fostering South-South cooperation while engaging with traditional economic powers. The bloc's emphasis on mutual benefit and inclusive growth has led to the formation of new alliances and partnerships, allowing them to assert their interests in various global economic forums, leading to significant changes in existing trade dynamics and power structures.

A critical aspect of BRICS' negotiation strategies lies in their concerted efforts to address key challenges facing developing economies, including fair representation in international financial institutions and the reform of global trade rules. Through strategic diplomacy and coalition-building, BRICS has endeavored to drive reforms that resonate with the aspirations of emerging economies, thereby reshaping the normative principles that govern international economic relations.

Moreover, the establishment of platforms such as the New Development Bank and the Contingent Reserve Arrangement has exemplified BRICS' commitment to setting up alternative institutions that provide greater financial stability and autonomy, thereby offering a viable counterbalance to the influence of established global financial entities.

In sum, the analysis of BRICS' unified negotiation strategies reveals a paradigm shift in global economic governance, with the bloc exerting increasing influence and redefining the norms and structures of international economic negotiations. As BRICS continues to articulate and assert its collective stance on global economic matters, it is poised to reshape the contours of international economic relations, compelling both traditional powers and emerging economies to adapt to a new geopolitical and economic order.

Long-term Economic Implications for Global Markets

The rapid emergence and sustained growth of the BRICS economies, comprising Brazil, Russia, India, China, and South Africa, have significantly altered the landscape of global markets. As these nations solidify their positions as economic powerhouses, the long-term implications for global markets are profound and multifaceted. One key implication is the shifting dynamics of trade and investment flows. With the rise of BRICS nations, traditional economic powerhouses have faced formidable competition in international markets. This has led to a rebalancing of global economic influence and trade patterns, causing existing market leaders to reassess their strategies to maintain their competitiveness.

Moreover, the increasing economic clout of BRICS nations has fostered a rise in South-South cooperation, leading to new models of economic partnership that bypass traditional Western-centric institutions. This trend has redefined the rules of engagement in global trade and investment, with BRICS nations exerting greater influence on shaping international economic governance frameworks. Consequently, the long-term implications for global markets include a gradual transformation of the existing economic order, as new players challenge established norms and institutions.

Another crucial implication stems from the growing interconnectedness of global financial markets. The ascendancy of BRICS economies has catalyzed the interconnectedness of capital flows, financial instruments, and investment opportunities. This has not only enhanced diversification prospects for investors worldwide but also led to a more integrated and resilient global financial system. However, it has also engendered complex interdependencies across markets, magnifying the impact of economic events in BRICS nations on global financial stability. Therefore, the long-term implications encompass a heightened need for effective risk management and collaborative regulatory frameworks to safeguard global financial stability amid increased interconnectedness.

Furthermore, the rising prominence of BRICS nations has prompted a reevaluation of global resource allocation and infrastructure development. Their growing demand for energy, raw materials, and infrastructure investment has driven fundamental shifts in global production and distribution networks. This has resulted in an intensified competition for resources, influencing the geopolitics of energy and commodities, and necessitating adaptations in global supply chains and logistics. Therefore, the long-term implications encompass a restructuring of global resource allocation and a recalibration of infrastructure investments to meet the evolving demands of emerging economies.

In conclusion, the sustained rise of BRICS economies presents enduring implications for global markets, spanning trade dynamics, financial interconnectedness, resource allocation, and geopolitical alignments. As these nations consolidate their positions as major economic actors, the ripple effects of their ascent will continue to reshape the contours of the global economy, necessitating adaptive strategies and collaborative frameworks to navigate the evolving landscape of global markets.

Future Predictions: Challenges and Opportunities for BRICS

As we look toward the future, the BRICS nations stand at a crucial juncture in shaping the global economic landscape. The trajectory of these emerging economies presents both challenges and opportunities that will significantly impact international trade, investment patterns, and geopolitical dynamics. One of the key challenges for BRICS lies in maintaining sustainable economic growth amidst increasing global competition and evolving market demands. While each member nation has made remarkable strides in expanding their influence, they must navigate through potential economic slowdowns, structural reforms, and external shocks that could impede their progress. Moreover, the diversification of their economies and reducing dependency on commodities exports will be imperative for long-term growth.

On the flip side, the rise of BRICS also presents a multitude of opportunities that could reshape the existing global economic order. With a combined GDP accounting for a significant portion of the world's economy, BRICS has the potential to become a formidable force in setting new standards for global trade and investment. By leveraging their collective strength, BRICS nations can emerge as influential players in international financial institutions and trade negotiations, potentially challenging the dominance of traditional economic powers. Furthermore, the strong focus on innovation, technological advancements, and sustainable development within the BRICS bloc could pave the way for groundbreaking collaborations and industry disruptions across various sectors, creating fresh opportunities for both domestic and international investors.

Nevertheless, as BRICS continues to ascend, they must address several pressing issues inherent to their individual economies and the collective alliance. These include improving governance structures, enhancing institutional frameworks, tackling income inequality, bolstering social and environmental sustainability, and fostering greater cooperation in addressing global challenges such as climate change and cybersecurity threats. Additionally, navigating geopolitical tensions and external pressures while maintaining internal unity and strategic solidarity will be critical for securing long-term success.

In conclusion, the future holds a mix of challenges and opportunities for BRICS nations as they position themselves as key players in the global economic landscape. Successfully addressing the multifaceted challenges and capitalizing on the abundant opportunities will define the path towards establishing a more equitable, inclusive, and resilient global economic order.

Conclusion: Implications for Global Economic Order

The rise of BRICS has significant implications for the global economic order. As these emerging economies continue to grow and expand their influence, the established economic powers will need to adapt to a new world dynamic. The increasing importance of the BRICS nations in shaping international economic policies and trade agreements cannot be overlooked. It is evident that the global economic landscape is undergoing a substantial transformation, with power dynamics shifting towards these emerging markets.

One of the key implications for the global economic order is the potential reconfiguration of international trade agreements and financial institutions. The influence of BRICS on these mechanisms is likely to challenge the traditional dominance of Western powers in setting the rules of global commerce. This could lead to a more balanced and inclusive approach to economic governance, with a greater representation of the interests of developing economies.

Moreover, the rise of BRICS may also lead to a more multipolar world, where economic power is more evenly distributed among different regions. This can create opportunities for collaboration and mutually beneficial partnerships across continents, fostering a more interconnected and interdependent global economy. However, it also poses challenges as existing structures and systems may need to accommodate the diverse perspectives and priorities of these emerging economies.

The implications for the global economic order extend beyond trade and finance. They also encompass geopolitical relationships, security arrangements, and developmental initiatives. The influence of BRICS on these aspects can potentially shape a new paradigm of global cooperation and competition, redefining traditional alliances and power dynamics.

In conclusion, the rise of BRICS holds profound implications for the global economic order. It signals a significant shift in the balance of economic influence and underscores the need for a more inclusive and adaptive approach to global economic governance. Embracing the opportunities and addressing the challenges presented by the growing impact of BRICS will be crucial in establishing a sustainable and equitable global economic order for the future.

CHAPTER

13

WESTERN ACCUSATIONS AGAINST CHINA

WESTERN ACCUSATIONS

The relationship between Western nations and China has been underpinned by a complex interplay of economic co-operation, geopolitical competition, and increasingly contentious trade relations. In recent years, Western nations, particularly the United States and some European countries, have levied a series of accusations against China, alleging a wide range of unfair trade practices, intellectual property theft, and non-compliance with global trading norms. These accusations have significantly strained diplomatic ties and led to an atmosphere of mistrust and suspicion. The central focus of these accusations revolves around alleged Chinese infringement upon intellectual property rights, purportedly costing Western businesses billions in lost revenues annually. Furthermore, Western nations have pointed to signifi-cant trade imbalances, questioning China's commitment to open and fair market practices and its adherence to international trade regulations. Additionally, concerns have been raised about China's state-led economic model, which some view as a form of unfair competition that distorts global markets. The ensuing economic tensions have also spilled over into political and security realms, casting a shadow over broader international relations. It is within this charged context that it becomes imperative to carefully examine and critically assess these accusations to discern their veracity and implications. This chapter seeks to provide a comprehensive analysis of the various accusations made by Western nations against China, evaluating their impact on global economic dynamics and international diplomacy.

Contextual Background of Accusations

The Western accusations against China arise from a complex and intricate backdrop entrenched in historical, economic, and political dynamics. It is essential to delve into the contextual background of these accusations to gain a comprehensive understanding of the multifaceted nature of the allegations. The roots of the accusations can be traced back to the significant shift in global economic power dynamics, where China's meteoric rise as an economic powerhouse has posed substantial challenges to the traditional dominance of Western nations. This shift has led to heightened competition, trade frictions, and geopolitical tensions, ultimately shaping the lens through which Western nations perceive China's actions. Moreover, historical incidents such as the Cold War era and ideological conflicts have contributed to the development of mutual suspicion and apprehension between China and the West, further exacerbating the context in which accusations are situated.

Analysis of Intellectual Property Theft Allegations

The accusations surrounding intellectual property theft have been a focal point in the ongoing trade and economic disputes between China and the Western nations, particularly the United States. The alleged theft of intellectual property has raised significant concerns regarding the fairness of trade practices and the protection of proprietary technologies. In analyzing these allegations, it is imperative to delve into the complexities of intellectual property laws, enforcement mechanisms, and the broader implications for global innovation and economic competition.

One facet of this analysis involves exploring the legal frameworks that govern intellectual property rights in China and assessing the extent to which these laws align with international standards. This entails an examination of China's legislative developments, judicial rulings, and efforts to enhance enforcement measures. Furthermore, it necessitates an appraisal of how intellectual property rights are perceived and safeguarded within China's evolving economic landscape.

Moreover, the analysis should encompass an evaluation of the evidence supporting the allegations of intellectual property theft. This requires a meticulous examination of case studies, industry reports, and empirical data to gauge the prevalence and impact of such illicit activities. By scrutinizing specific instances of alleged intellectual property theft, one can ascertain the modus operandi of infringing entities, the industries most affected, and the repercussions faced by victimized companies.

In addition, this section should critically assess the broader implications of intellectual property theft on innovation, technological progress, and global competitiveness. It is essential to elucidate how such misappropriation may stifle incentive structures for research and development, deter foreign investment, and distort market dynamics. Furthermore, it is vital to explore the potential spillover effects on cross-border collaborations, as well as the intricacies of navigating intellectual property disputes within a transnational context.

Ultimately, a comprehensive analysis of intellectual property theft allegations necessitates a holistic examination of legal, economic, and strategic dimensions. By elucidating the nuances of these allegations, this analysis aims to provide a nuanced understanding of the multifaceted nature of intellectual property protection and its profound ramifications on the international economic landscape.

Trade Imbalances: Scrutiny and Impact

Trade imbalances have been a subject of intense scrutiny in the global economic arena, particularly concerning the relationship between the United States and China. These imbalances arise when a country's exports exceed its imports, leading to a surplus in its trade balance, or when imports surpass exports, creating a deficit. The impact of trade imbalances can be profound, affecting various sectors of the economy and raising concerns among policymakers and economists alike.

At the heart of the debate surrounding trade imbalances is the perceived effect on employment. Critics argue that persistent trade deficits, especially those with a single trading partner like China, can lead to job losses in industries facing increased competition from cheaper imported goods. This has sparked contentious discussions about the outsourcing of jobs and the decline of domestic manufacturing in the United States, leading to broader debates about protectionist measures and the impact on the labor market.

Moreover, trade imbalances also carry implications for currency valuations and exchange rates. Large trade surpluses, such as those witnessed in Chinese trade relationships, can result in upward pressure on China's currency, the renminbi, relative to other currencies like the U.S. dollar. This, in turn, can affect the competitiveness of Chinese exports and influence global financial markets, prompting concerns about currency manipulation and its broader impact on international trade dynamics.

In addition to these macroeconomic consequences, trade imbalances can influence the overall stability of global financial systems. Excessive reliance on foreign borrowing to finance trade deficits can leave countries vulnerable to sudden shifts in investor confidence or changes in the availability of credit, potentially leading to financial crises and economic turmoil. This vulnerability has drawn attention to the need for more sustainable trade practices and policies that promote a balanced and mutually beneficial trading environment.

The scrutiny of trade imbalances inevitably extends to the geopolitical realm, with implications for diplomatic relations, international cooperation, and treaty negotiations. As pivotal players in the global economy, the United States and China navigate a complex landscape of trade intricacies, seeking to address imbalances while fostering a constructive and collaborative trade environment. The interplay of economic interests, political considerations, and strategic objectives underscores the multifaceted nature of addressing trade imbalances on a global scale.

In conclusion, the assessment of trade imbalances and their impacts demands a comprehensive understanding of their underlying causes, economic repercussions, and broader significance within the evolving dynamics of global trade. Addressing these imbalances requires prudent policy frameworks, diplomatic engagements, and cooperative efforts among nations to cultivate a more equitable and sustainable global trading system.

Unfair Trade Practices: Definition and Examples

The concept of unfair trade practices encompasses a range of behaviors that deviate from the principles of fair competition in the global marketplace. These practices are often employed to gain an unfair advantage over competitors or trading partners, thereby distorting the economic playing field. One prevalent example of unfair trade practices is the manipulation of currency exchange rates to artificially lower the cost of exports, making them more competitive in foreign markets. This not only undermines the principles of free and fair trade but also results in significant trade imbalances and disadvantages for countries operating under more transparent currency regimes.

Another common form of unfair trade practice involves the dumping of goods into foreign markets at below-market prices, often subsidized by the government. Such predatory pricing strategies not only destabilize local industries but also lead to increased barriers for domestic producers, creating an uneven landscape for international trade. In addition, intellectual property theft and forced technology transfer stand as egregious violations of fair trade principles, where companies are coerced into sharing proprietary knowledge in exchange for market access in foreign territories.

Furthermore, the exploitation of labor through substandard working conditions and non-compliance with international labor standards represents another facet of unfair trade practices. By undercutting production costs through unethical labor practices, companies gain an unfair competitive edge while perpetuating human rights abuses and compromising the well-being of workers. Additionally, the use of non-tariff barriers such as discriminatory regulations, import restrictions, and arbitrary standards serve as covert mechanisms for disadvantaging foreign competitors.

It is critical to recognize that unfair trade practices not only disrupt the equilibrium of global trade but also pose serious challenges to the stability and integrity of the international economic order. Adhering to the principles of fair and equitable trade is paramount for fostering mutually beneficial relationships among nations and ensuring sustainable development. Addressing these practices requires collective action, robust regulatory frameworks, and transparent enforcement mechanisms to uphold the integrity of international trade and promote a level playing field for all participants.

Methodology for Evaluating the Validity of Accusations

In the realm of international trade, allegations of unfair practices have become prevalent, often inciting discord and controversy. The methodology for evaluating the validity of such accusations is a rigorous process that demands precision and impartial analysis. Central to this inquiry is the need for comprehensive assessments that delve into various facets of the accused party's behavior. To begin with, it is essential to conduct meticulous research concerning the specific allegations being leveled against the accused. This involves scrutinizing trade data, market trends, and regulatory frameworks to gain a nuanced understanding of the circumstances in question. Moreover, an examination of relevant legal agreements and international trade laws should be undertaken to ascertain whether the accused party has violated established regulations. Another critical component of the methodology involves engaging in bilateral or multilateral dialogues between the accuser and the accused. This provides an opportunity for both parties to present their perspectives, exchange evidence, and engage in constructive discourse aimed at resolving the accusations. Furthermore, independent third-party investigations can play a pivotal role in evaluating the veracity of the allegations. These inquiries encompass forensic analyses, cross-referencing of financial records, and on-the-ground inspections to validate or debunk the claims at hand. It is imperative to incorporate a multidisciplinary approach, drawing upon legal, economic, and geopolitical expertise to ensure a well-rounded evaluation. Additionally, the assessment of broader macroeconomic factors, such as currency manipulation or state subsidies, is indispensable in adjudicating the fairness of trade practices. The adoption of a holistic perspective that considers the socio-political contexts within which alleged malpractices transpire is also vital. Ultimately, the methodology for evaluating these allegations necessitates an unwavering commitment to procedural integrity, adherence to international legal frameworks, and the pursuit of equitable resolutions. By employing these robust methodologies, the international community can strive towards fostering a fairer and more transparent global trade environment, thereby mitigating tensions stemming from unfounded allegations while addressing legitimate concerns with clarity and objectivity.

Case Studies: Dissecting Notable Accusations

In dissecting notable accusations against China, it is imperative to conduct thorough case studies to understand the complexity and nuances involved in such allegations. One prominent area of focus involves intellectual property theft, where numerous high-profile cases have garnered international attention. By delving into these cases, we can gain insights into the mechanics and implications of intellectual property theft, shedding light on whether the accusations against China hold merit. Furthermore, scrutinizing trade imbalances and unfair trade practices presents a compelling avenue for case studies. Examining specific trade disputes and their respective outcomes can provide valuable perspectives on the impact of these accusations on global trade dynamics. Moreover, conducting in-depth case studies enables a comprehensive evaluation of the broader economic and geopolitical ramifications of such allegations. By analyzing specific instances, we aim to offer a nuanced understanding of how these accusations have influenced international relations and affected diplomatic ties between Western nations and China. These case studies will serve as essential tools for policymakers, businesses, and scholars to navigate the complex landscape of international accusations and their implications, fostering informed decision-making and constructive dialogue.

Impact of Accusations on International Relations

The impact of accusations against China from Western countries has extended beyond the realm of economics, with significant reverberations in the arena of international relations. The diplomatic fallout stemming from these accusations has been felt across multiple dimensions, including trade negotiations, geopolitical alignments, and global cooperation efforts. These accusations have led to heightened tensions and strained relationships between China and various Western powers, creating an atmosphere of distrust and skepticism in diplomatic discussions and international forums. As a result, the ability to collaborate on shared challenges, such as climate change, global health crises, and security issues, has been impeded by the erosion of trust stemming from these economic accusations. Furthermore, the accusations have triggered retaliatory measures and counter-accusations from China, fuelling a cycle of escalating rhetoric and hostility that undermines the prospects for constructive dialogue and diplomacy. In addition, the perceived lack of fair treatment and respect in international discourse has fueled a sense of injustice and alienation among Chinese policymakers and the broader populace, potentially shaping their attitudes toward engaging with the international community. Beyond specific bilateral relations, the accusations have also affected multilateral platforms and institutions, with tensions spilling over into debates within organizations such as the World Trade Organization and impacting the formulation of global economic regulations. The fragmentation of consensus and cooperation at the international level due to these accusations has weakened the effectiveness of global governance and hindered efforts to address pressing global challenges collectively. Moreover, the increasing polarization and adversarial posturing resulting from these accusations have complicated the prospects for finding common ground on a range of issues, undermining the stability and predictability of the international order. As key stakeholders engage in a battle of narratives and perceptions, the broader fabric of international relations bears the brunt of this strain, jeopardizing the prospects for a more harmonious and collaborative global landscape. Thus, it is imperative to recognize and address the adverse ramifications of these accusations on international relations, seeking avenues for constructive dialogue, mutual understanding, and restoring trust among nations.

Comparative Analysis: Accusations Versus Reality

In analyzing the Western accusations against China, it is imperative to conduct a comparative analysis between the claims made and the actual reality. This process involves an in-depth investigation into each accusation, juxtaposed with factual evidence and contextual understanding. The objective is to discern the veracity of the allegations and ascertain their impact on international relations. A systematic approach will be adopted to ensure a comprehensive examination of each accusation.

The first step in the comparative analysis is to identify the specific accusations leveled against China by Western entities. These may include allegations of intellectual property theft, unfair trade practices, currency manipulation, and technology transfer coercion, among others. Once the accusations are delineated, a thorough exploration of the reality underlying each claim must be pursued. This involves delving into empirical data, historical contexts, and legal frameworks to provide a nuanced interpretation.

Subsequently, it is essential to evaluate the scope and impact of each accusation on bilateral and multilateral relationships. By elucidating the repercussions of these accusations on trade agreements, diplomatic engagements, and global economic dynamics, a deeper understanding of their significance can be attained. Moreover, a comparative assessment of the responses from both the Western accusers and Chinese authorities must be meticulously examined to gauge the trajectory of these contentions.

Furthermore, the comparative analysis necessitates an exploration of precedents and case studies wherein similar accusations were repudiated or substantiated. By drawing parallels with historical instances, such as trade disputes and intellectual property litigations, valuable insights can be gleaned to fortify the comparative analysis. This process enables a comprehensive understanding of the evolving nature of international trade dynamics and the implications of contentious accusations on the global economic order.

Ultimately, the comparative analysis seeks to offer a balanced and informed perspective on the veracity of the Western accusations against China. It endeavors to transcend unilateral narratives and engender a holistic comprehension of the complex entwinement of economic interests and geopolitical dynamics. By scrutinizing the accusations vis-a-vis empirical realities, this analysis aims to contribute to a more equitable and judicious discourse surrounding international economic relations and co-operation.

Conclusion and Implications

The detailed comparative analysis conducted in the preceding section sheds light on the complexities of Western accusations against China. While it is crucial to acknowledge instances where China has indeed engaged in unfair trade practices or intellectual property theft, it is equally important to approach these accusations with a balanced perspective. Over the years, the narrative surrounding China's economic practices has often been sensationalized, leading to heightened tension between China and the Western world. As we conclude this exploration, it becomes evident that addressing these accusations requires a multi-faceted approach that considers geopolitical, economic, and diplomatic dimensions.

Firstly, from an economic standpoint, it is imperative for both Western countries and China to engage in transparent dialogue and negotiation, aligning their interests to foster greater collaboration. By establishing clear protocols for intellectual property protection and fair trade, both parties can work towards a more equitable economic landscape. Additionally, through a mutual commitment to addressing trade imbalances and unfair practices, the potential for constructive partnerships and sustained economic growth can be realized.

Moreover, from a diplomatic standpoint, it is essential for governments and international organizations to initiate meaningful dialogue aimed at addressing these accusations in a manner that respects the sovereignty and identity of each nation involved. International bodies such as the World Trade Organization can play a pivotal role in facilitating discussions and mediating disputes to prevent escalations that could harm global economic stability. By promoting cooperation and mutual understanding, the international community can strive towards the resolution of issues pertaining to accusations against China and pave the way for enhanced collaboration.

Furthermore, the implications of effectively managing these accusations extend beyond the economic and diplomatic realms. Successfully navigating these challenges can set a precedent for how nations navigate complex geopolitical relationships, fostering an environment of trust and cooperation that transcends individual grievances. Through a collective commitment to dialogue and transparency, countries can forge partnerships based on mutual respect, leading to a more harmonious global landscape. The implications carry significant weight, not just for China and Western nations, but for the broader international community as a whole.

CHINA'S PERSPECTIVE ON ADAPTATION

INTRODUCTION: CHINA'S RESPONSE TO EXTERNAL PRESSURES

China's economic evolution has often been viewed through the lens of non-conformity to Western economic practices and norms. As the global economic landscape continues to be shaped by international criticisms and pressures for reforms, China's response to these external influences becomes a matter of significant interest and analysis. The initial reaction of China to international criticism and pressure for economic changes was characterized by a complex interplay of historical context, ideological foundations, and a deep-rooted commitment to preserving its sovereignty and unique development path. China's steadfast adherence to its own economic model has faced persistent scrutiny from the Western world, leading to a dynamic and at times contentious dialogue between China and the global community. It is essential to delve into the nuances of this response, acknowledging the multifaceted dimensions of China's economic policies and the underlying factors that have shaped its approach to external pressures. Understanding the historical context within which China's economic policies were formulated provides crucial insights into the driving forces behind its resistance to conforming to Western economic paradigms. Moreover, an in-depth examination of China's ideological foundations sheds light on the principles that underpin its economic decision-making, highlighting the intrinsic motivations that guide its response to external pressures. This section aims to unravel the complexities of China's response to international criticisms and pressures, exploring the intricate tapestry of historical, ideological, and strategic elements that have influenced its stance in the face of evolving global dynamics.

Historical Context of Non-Conformity

Throughout its history, China has exhibited a consistent stance of non-conformity to external pressures and influence, rooted in a deep historical context. From the early periods of dynastic rule to the modern era, China's approach to economic and political independence has been shaped by a complex interplay of factors. One pivotal element is the concept of sovereignty and the perceived need to safeguard it against foreign interference. The legacy of imperial China, with its emphasis on self-sufficiency and centralized governance, laid the groundwork for the nation's enduring commitment to chart its course on its own terms. Additionally, the trauma of colonial subjugation during the 19th and early 20th centuries further reinforced China's resolve to assert its autonomy and resist external dictates. This historical backdrop illuminates the deep-seated motivations underlying China's non-conformist stance. Moreover, the experiences of rapid industrialization and socialist development under Mao Zedong's leadership engendered a sense of national pride and self-reliance. This period saw China pursuing a unique path of economic and political transformation, distinct from Western models, fostering an enduring ethos of autonomy and resilience. The tumultuous events of the 20th century, including the Chinese Civil War, the Second Sino-Japanese War, and the Cultural Revolution, instilled in the Chinese populace a steadfast determination to forge their destiny without succumbing to external pressures. As such, the historical context of non-conformity is deeply embedded in China's national identity, profoundly influencing its approach to economic adaptation and global engagement. This rich historical tapestry provides critical insights into China's continued dedication to upholding its principles amidst evolving international dynamics, defining its contemporary interactions with the global community.

Theoretical Foundations of China's Economic Independence

Amidst the evolving landscape of global economic dynamics, China has strived to establish and fortify its economic independence through a strategic implementation of various theoretical constructs. At the core of this endeavor lies the meticulous adoption and adaptation of economic theories that resonate with the unique socio-political fabric of the nation. One such foundational framework is rooted in the principles of socialist market economy, which amalgamates central planning with market mechanisms to empower the state to guide and regulate economic activities while also allowing market forces to play a decisive role in resource allocation. This dualistic approach embraces the essence of socialism while harnessing the dynamism of market-oriented policies, enabling China to chart an autonomous economic pathway. Furthermore, the concept of self-reliance has been deeply ingrained in China's economic ideology, epitomized by Deng Xiaoping's doctrine of 'Socialism with Chinese Characteristics'. This ideology emphasizes the imperative for China to rely on its own strength and resources to propel economic growth and development, thereby establishing a robust foundation for economic independence. Additionally, the principle of 'Harmonious Society' serves as a guiding philosophy, aiming to alleviate social disparities and foster balanced development, aligning with the pursuit of self-sufficiency and resilience. In juxtaposition with prevalent Western economic paradigms, these theoretical underpinnings underscore China's distinctive approach to economic policy-making and exemplify the underpinning rationale behind the nation's steadfast pursuit of economic sovereignty. Leveraging these theoretical frameworks, China endeavors to assert its autonomy and resilience amidst global economic interdependencies, thereby shaping a paradigm that advocates for assertive adaptation and independent progression within the contemporary economic milieu.

Analysis of Western Demands on China's Economic Practices

As a global economic powerhouse, China has often found itself at odds with Western demands regarding its economic practices. The juxtaposition of China's state-led capitalist model against the Western ideology of free-market capitalism has led to numerous conflicts and negotiations in international forums.

At the core of these conflicts lies the issue of market access and fair competition. Western countries have consistently demanded that China open up its markets further, reduce trade barriers, and provide a more level playing field for foreign companies. This demand stems from the perception that China's protectionist policies unfairly disadvantage Western firms and create an uneven global economic landscape.

Another major point of contention is intellectual property rights. Western nations have continuously pressed China to strengthen its legal framework for protecting intellectual property, citing instances of widespread counterfeiting and patent infringement. The lack of robust enforcement measures within China has led to concerns about technology transfer and innovation theft, exacerbating tensions between China and Western economies.

Furthermore, issues surrounding currency manipulation and exchange rate policies have contributed to friction between China and Western powers. Accusations of intentionally devaluing its currency to gain an unfair trade advantage have been recurrent, prompting heated debates and calls for greater transparency and adherence to international currency standards.

The demands on environmental standards and labor practices also feature prominently in the discourse. Western entities have urged China to align its environmental regulations and labor laws with international norms, emphasizing the need for sustainable development and improved working conditions. Disputes over subsidies to state-owned enterprises and allegations of dumping excess production capacity have further intensified the scrutiny toward China's economic practices.

Despite the confrontational nature of these demands, there exist avenues for constructive dialogue and mutual understanding. Achieving a balance between national autonomy and global economic integration remains a complex yet critical challenge for China. By carefully navigating these demands and formulating responses rooted in pragmatism and cooperation, China can contribute to a more harmonious and equitable global economic order.

Case Studies: Successes of Indigenous Economic Policies

China's economic growth and development have often been the subject of global attention and scrutiny. One of the key elements that have contributed to China's remarkable transformation has been its indigenous economic policies. These policies, designed to fit with the unique cultural and historical context of China, have yielded significant successes that offer valuable insights for the global economic community.

A prominent case study of successful indigenous economic policy is the development of China's renewable energy sector. As a response to environmental challenges and increasing energy demands, China implemented policies aimed at promoting the use of clean and renewable energy sources. The results have been impressive, with China now being a global leader in renewable energy production and technology innovation. This success not only addresses domestic environmental concerns but also positions China as a key player in the global transition towards sustainable energy.

Another compelling case study lies in China's agricultural modernization efforts. By leveraging traditional farming techniques alongside modern technological advancements, China has achieved significant improvements in agricultural productivity and food security. Through targeted policies and investments, China has effectively lifted millions out of poverty and established itself as a major contributor to global food production and distribution.

Additionally, China's government-led industrial policies have played a pivotal role in fostering the growth of strategic industries such as high-speed rail, telecommunications, and e-commerce. These initiatives, tailored to meet China's specific developmental needs, have propelled the nation to the forefront of global technological advancement and economic competitiveness.

Moreover, the Belt and Road Initiative (BRI) stands as a testament to China's proactive approach to building economic ties and infrastructure development across continents. By aligning with the historical Silk Road trade routes, China's pursuit of the BRI reflects a deep understanding of its own geopolitical and economic advantages, forging new pathways for international trade and connectivity.

The successes of these indigenous economic policies in China showcase the importance of adapting strategies to fit local contexts and traditions. They offer valuable lessons for other nations seeking sustainable development and economic growth, emphasizing the significance of tailoring policies to address specific needs and leverage inherent strengths. As global economic dynamics continue to evolve, the case studies of China's indigenous economic policies serve as a unique source of inspiration and guidance for crafting effective and enduring developmental strategies worldwide.

Innovations in Technology and Sustainable Development

China has showcased a remarkable commitment to sustainable development through the integration of innovative technologies across various sectors. The nation's strategic investments in research and development have significantly contributed to the realization of sustainable practices within its economic framework. One prominent area of emphasis has been the renewable energy sector. China's implementation of cutting-edge technologies in solar and wind power has fueled substantial advancements, positioning the country as a global leader in clean energy production and utilization.

Furthermore, China's ambitious initiatives extend beyond the energy sector, encompassing diverse fields such as transportation, agriculture, and urban planning. The widespread deployment of electric vehicles, high-speed rail networks, and smart infrastructure exemplifies the nation's dedication to integrating technological innovations for environmental sustainability and resource efficiency. These endeavors not only bolster China's domestic development but also offer valuable insights and solutions for global challenges pertaining to climate change and ecological preservation.

In alignment with sustainable development goals, China has embraced the concept of the circular economy, forging a transition from traditional linear production models to more regenerative and resource-conserving approaches. Through the effective utilization of digitalization, big data, and artificial intelligence, China has been instrumental in optimizing resource allocation, waste management, and environmental conservation efforts. The comprehensive application of advanced technology not only mitigates ecological impacts but also fosters economic resilience and long-term viability.

Moreover, China's adherence to sustainable development goes beyond the realm of technology, extending to social innovation and community engagement. The incorporation of green practices within everyday lifestyles and the promotion of eco-consciousness among citizens reflect the country's holistic approach towards fostering a sustainable society. Notably, collaborative partnerships between government institutions, private enterprises, and academic entities have facilitated the seamless integration of innovative solutions into societal frameworks, cultivating a culture of sustainability and responsibility.

Ultimately, China's unwavering commitment to technological innovations and sustainable development serves as a testament to its proactive stance in addressing contemporary environmental challenges. By harnessing the transformative power of advanced technologies and embracing progressive paradigms of sustainable growth, China continues to set formidable precedents for global sustainability and pave the way for a harmonious coexistence between economic progress and environmental preservation.

Sociopolitical Stability and Public Support

The sociopolitical stability of a nation plays a pivotal role in shaping its economic development. In the context of China, the government's commitment to maintaining stability has been a key factor in the country's rapid economic growth. The Chinese leadership has demonstrated a firm determination to ensure social harmony and maintain political stability, which has provided a conducive environment for sustainable economic progress. This stability has not only fostered public confidence in the government's ability to manage the economy but has also encouraged domestic and international investment. Moreover, the government's emphasis on policies that prioritize poverty alleviation and social welfare programs has contributed to the overall stability of the society by addressing economic disparities and promoting equal opportunities. Additionally, China's efforts to address environmental concerns and promote sustainable development have garnered public support and strengthened the country's social fabric. The government's initiatives to improve living standards, urban infrastructure, and healthcare services have further bolstered the public's trust in the state and its economic strategies. Furthermore, China's effective management of social order and security has also had a positive impact on the investment climate, encouraging businesses to operate confidently within the country. All these factors combined have created a virtuous cycle of stability and confidence, providing a robust foundation for sustained economic growth and prosperity. As China continues to navigate the complexities of global economic dynamics, the maintenance of sociopolitical stability and garnering public support remains integral to the country's adaptive strategies. Understanding the interplay between economic development and sociopolitical stability is crucial not only for China but also for the broader global community. By analyzing China's unique approach to fostering stability and public support, valuable insights can be gained for shaping more inclusive and sustainable economic models across the world.

Comparative Analysis with Western Economic Challenges

As China's economic model continues to evolve, it becomes increasingly important to juxtapose its challenges and successes with those of Western economies. In examining the comparative economic challenges, it is evident that China and the West face distinct but interconnected sets of issues. One crucial aspect is the differing approaches to fiscal and monetary policies, where China's state-led model contrasts sharply with the market-driven approach adopted by Western countries. This fundamental difference gives rise to varying responses to financial crises, inflation, and unemployment rates. Additionally, the divergent regulatory frameworks in both systems significantly impact their abilities to navigate global economic turbulence. While the Western neoliberal paradigm emphasizes individualism and deregulation, China's state capitalism prioritizes collective economic progress and robust controls. The debate surrounding the balance between free-market principles and state intervention takes center stage in this comparative analysis, shedding light on contrasting economic ideologies and their implications for sustainable development. Furthermore, the resilience of China's economic system in weathering global shocks raises questions about the adaptability of Western economies to systemic challenges. With

China's rapid advancements in technology and innovation, there is a growing concern about whether Western counterparts can compete effectively and sustainably in the digital age. This comparative analysis also delves into the environmental sustainability strategies of both entities, highlighting the contrast between China's centralized green initiatives and the decentralized nature of Western environmental policies. Finally, the examination of income inequality, social welfare provisions, and labor market structures uncovers disparities and commonalities in addressing societal well-being. By dissecting these multifaceted dimensions of economic challenges, this comparison provides valuable insights into the opportunities and obstacles for mutual learning and collaboration between China and the West, thereby setting the stage for an enriched international economic landscape.

Future Projections: Adapting Within Own Terms

As China continues to navigate the complexities of the global economic landscape, it is imperative to project the trajectory of its own economic adaptation within the constructs of its indigenous policies and practices. The future projections for China's economic adaptation rest on the country's ability to leverage its rich history, diverse culture, and evolving technological advancements to carve a unique path that aligns with its national interests while contributing to global economic stability. With the Western economic challenges serving as a compelling backdrop, China seeks to chart a course that embraces both innovation and preservation of its core values. One key aspect of these future projections revolves around the strategic implementation of sustainable development practices that not only foster economic growth but also prioritize environmental conservation and social well-being. China's emphasis on integrating cutting-edge technology and green initiatives sets the stage for a forward-looking approach to economic adaptation that has ripple effects in shaping the global economic landscape. Moreover, China's projection entails a comprehensive analysis of the geopolitical shifts and trade dynamics, underpinning the need for a balanced and pragmatic approach to external economic partnerships and domestic autonomy. As the country anticipates its future role in the global economic arena, ensuring sociopolitical stability and garnering public support remains pivotal. The government's proactive engagement with the citizens, businesses, and academia will drive a collective vision that resonates with the aspirations and needs of the population, positioning China for sustainable and inclusive economic adaptation. In navigating future projections, China recognizes the importance of synergy between indigenous economic practices and global economic integration. By harnessing its unique blend of tradition and modernity, China aims to foster an adaptive economic model that not only withstands external pressures but also propels global economic relations towards mutually beneficial outcomes. The overarching implication of China's future projections transcends the nation's borders, offering a paradigm for other emerging economies and established powers to recalibrate their approaches within the evolving economic landscape. As China strives to adapt within its own terms, it paves the way for a new narrative of economic cooperation and coexistence, redefining the contours of global economic relations.

Summary and Implications for Global Economic Relations

As China continues to chart its own course in economic development, the implications for global economic relations are profound. The country's sustained focus on indigenous innovation, technological advancement, and sustainable growth presents a formidable challenge to the established economic order dominated by Western powers. By asserting its independence and adapting within its own terms, China has not only reshaped its domestic landscape but has also disrupted traditional paradigms of global economic relations.

Firstly, the summary of China's approach to adaptation emphasizes its determination to pursue economic development that is rooted in its unique historical, cultural, and political context. This distinction underscores the need for other nations and international organizations to recognize and respect diverse models of economic progress, thereby fostering a more inclusive and pluralistic global economic framework.

Moreover, the implications for global economic relations extend beyond mere competition between China and other major economies. China's unwavering commitment to sustainability and responsible resource management sets an example for the world at large, encouraging a reevaluation of existing economic practices and promoting greater environmental consciousness across all nations.

Furthermore, China's emphasis on social and political stability as a crucial underpinning of its economic strategy offers a valuable lesson for global economic relations. By prioritizing cohesiveness and public support, China demonstrates the interconnected nature of economic well-being and societal harmony, challenging conventional narratives that prioritize economic growth at the expense of social welfare.

Considering these implications, it becomes evident that the rise of China and its distinctive approach to economic adaptation provide an opportunity for constructive dialogue and collaboration among nations. Rather than viewing China's success as a threat to existing economic orders, global actors should embrace the chance to learn from and engage with China's experiences, leveraging shared insights to address common economic challenges and foster mutual understanding.

In conclusion, the summary of China's perspective on adaptation underscores the transformative potential of the country's economic trajectory and its implications for global economic relations. By respecting diversity, prioritizing sustainability, and emphasizing social cohesion, China's approach invites the international community to reimagine the contours of economic cooperation and shape a more inclusive and harmonious global economic landscape.

SUSTAINABILITY ISSUES IN THE U.S. ECONOMIC MODEL

OVERVIEW OF THE CURRENT U.S. ECONOMIC MODEL

The current U.S. economic model is a complex amalgamation of market forces, government regulations, and international trade dynamics. It has served as a centerpiece of global capitalism and economic prosperity for decades, characterized by its emphasis on innovation, entrepreneurship, and consumer-driven consumption. Evaluated within a global context, the U.S. economic system has demonstrated remarkable resilience and adaptability, navigating through various economic crises and geopolitical shifts. Its prominence in international trade, financial markets, and technological advancements has bolstered its influence and standing in the global economic arena. However, this model also faces scrutiny and challenges. Criticisms center around sustainability concerns, income inequality, and the environmental impact of relentless growth and consumption. The effectiveness of the U.S. economic paradigm is being questioned in light of evolving global economic, social, and environmental dynamics. As we delve deeper into assessing the dynamism and functionality of the U.S. economic model, it becomes imperative to weigh its strengths against potential vulnerabilities and shortcomings, thereby illuminating the critical evaluation of its role and impact in the rapidly changing global economic landscape.

Defining Sustainability in Economic Terms

Sustainability, in the context of the U.S. economic model, represents the capacity to meet the needs of the present without compromising the ability of future generations to meet their own needs. It encompasses various dimensions, including environmental, social, and economic considerations. From an economic standpoint, sustainability involves managing resources and economic activities in a way that ensures long-term viability and stability. This extends beyond traditional profit-driven approaches to encompass broader societal and environmental impacts. The concept of sustainability emphasizes responsible resource utilization, equitable distribution of wealth, and the mitigation of negative externalities. In essence, it seeks to balance economic growth with environmental protection and social well-being. Defining sustainability in economic terms requires a holistic approach that considers the interconnectedness of economic activities, environmental resources, and societal welfare. It involves assessing the impacts of economic decisions on natural ecosystems, human communities, and future generations. Economic sustainability strives to maintain a healthy economy while preserving the environment and supporting social equity. Achieving economic sustainability necessitates measuring progress using indicators that go beyond traditional economic metrics, such as GDP growth. These indicators may include measures of resource efficiency, income distribution, social inclusion, and environmental quality. By incorporating these factors, a more comprehensive understanding of economic performance can be gained, which aligns with sustainable development goals. Additionally, economic sustainability involves fostering innovation and technological advancements that promote efficiency, reduce waste, and minimize environmental harm. This entails encouraging businesses and industries to adopt sustainable practices and invest in renewable energy sources, eco-friendly technologies, and circular economy models. Furthermore, promoting economic sustainability requires aligning policies and regulations to incentivize responsible behaviors while discouraging unsustainable practices. This may involve implementing carbon pricing mechanisms, establishing environmental standards, and providing support for sustainable business initiatives. Governments, businesses, and civil society all play critical roles in advancing economic sustainability through collaboration, transparency, and accountability. Through collective efforts, it becomes possible to transition toward a more sustainable economic model that safeguards the well-being of current and future generations.

Critical Analysis of Environmental Impacts

The critical analysis of environmental impacts within the U.S. economic model reveals a complex interplay between industrial growth, resource utilization, and ecological consequences. This section seeks to examine the various dimensions through which economic activities exert pressure on the environment and natural resources. It starts by delving into the historical evolution of environmental policies and the ways in which they have shaped economic practices. From there, it scrutinizes the impact of industrialization, urbanization, and agricultural intensification on ecosystems, air quality, and water resources. Moreover, it evaluates the challenges associated with waste management, pollution control, and climate change mitigation efforts. Through a comprehensive examination of these factors, this analysis aims to highlight the systemic nature of environmental degradation as an inherent component of the U.S. economic model. Addressing these challenges requires a multifaceted approach that encompasses regulatory frameworks, technological innovations, public awareness campaigns, and international cooperation. Furthermore, this section underscores the urgent need for integrating sustainable development principles into economic decision-making processes to mitigate the adverse effects on the environment. By critically assessing the environmental impacts of the U.S. economic model, this discussion endeavors to shed light on the imperative for recalibrating economic strategies in a manner that prioritizes the preservation and restoration of environmental integrity.

Social Inequalities and Economic Sustainability

Social inequalities perpetuate significant challenges to the achievement of economic sustainability within the United States. The distribution of wealth and resources among different social groups plays a pivotal role in determining the resilience and longevity of the economic model. At present, disparities in income, access to education, healthcare, and job opportunities continue to widen the gap between the affluent and the marginalized segments of society. This exacerbates social tensions and undermines the overall stability and sustainability of the economy.

Addressing these issues is essential for fostering a more robust and enduring economic framework.

Furthermore, the persistent inequality within the U.S. population has detrimental effects on consumer spending patterns, as it limits the purchasing power of a significant portion of the populace. This, in turn, impacts demand for goods and services, hindering overall economic growth. Moreover, social inequalities can lead to reduced social cohesion, decreased trust in institutions, and heightened political instability, all of which have adverse effects on the sustainable economic development of the nation.

From a professional perspective, it becomes evident that achieving economic sustainability necessitates a comprehensive approach to mitigating social inequalities. Policy initiatives aimed at narrowing the wealth and opportunity gap through progressive taxation, targeted social welfare programs, and investment in education and training can contribute to a more equitable distribution of wealth and support long-term economic growth. Additionally, fostering an inclusive and diverse workforce while promoting equal employment opportunities can enhance productivity and innovation, thereby positively impacting economic sustainability.

Given these considerations, it is imperative for policymakers, industry leaders, and stakeholders to recognize the pivotal connection between social inequalities and economic sustainability. Prioritizing initiatives that bridge these gaps and promote a more equitable society will not only bolster the economic prospects of the nation but also lay the foundation for a more resilient and sustainable economic model that benefits all members of society.

Economic Policies and Long-term Growth

In assessing the long-term sustainability of the U.S. economic model, it is imperative to evaluate the role of economic policies in shaping future growth prospects. Economic policies play a crucial role in steering the trajectory of a nation's economy, influencing key indicators such as employment rates, inflation, productivity, and overall economic stability. Moreover, a careful examination of economic policies can shed light on their alignment with sustainable development goals and their potential impact on long-term growth. Policymakers must navigate the complexities of balancing short-term economic demands with the imperative of safeguarding resources for future generations. Engaging in forward-thinking economic policies that prioritize environmental preservation, social equity, and technological innovation is essential for ensuring sustainable long-term growth. A critical aspect of promoting long-term economic growth involves fostering an environment conducive to investment, entrepreneurship, and technological advancement. Proactive policies aimed at incentivizing research and development, promoting access to capital for small and medium-sized enterprises, and fostering a culture of innovation can drive sustained economic growth. Additionally, the cultivation of a skilled workforce through strategic education and training initiatives is instrumental in enhancing a nation's competitiveness and adaptive capacity in the global economic landscape. Furthermore, the formulation of policies that encourage sustainable consumption and production patterns contributes to mitigating environmental degradation and fortifying the resilience of the economy. Governments should prioritize investments in infrastructure, renewable energy, and sustainable technologies, thereby laying the groundwork for a more sustainable and efficient economic system. Striking a balance between economic growth and ecological integrity necessitates the integration of environmental considerations into policy frameworks. By implementing measures that internalize externalities, such as carbon pricing and regulations that enhance resource efficiency, nations can promote sustainable growth while safeguarding natural ecosystems. This holistic approach to economic policymaking encompasses not only fostering robust economic performance but also ensuring that growth is compatible with the preservation of ecosystems and the well-being of present and future generations. Ultimately, the formulation and implementation of forward-looking economic policies are pivotal in charting a course toward long-term growth that is harmonious with social, environmental, and economic considerations.

Innovations in Sustainable Economic Practices

Innovations in sustainable economic practices are fundamental to addressing the increasingly urgent global challenges of climate change, resource depletion, and environmental degradation. This section explores how innovative approaches and technologies are revolutionizing the ways in which businesses and economies operate while mitigating their impacts on the environment. One of the key areas of innovation is the development of renewable energy sources. Advancements in solar, wind, and hydroelectric power have significantly reduced reliance on fossil fuels, offering cleaner and more sustainable alternatives for meeting energy demands. Additionally, the integration of smart grid technologies and energy storage solutions has enhanced the efficiency and reliability of renewable energy systems, paving the way for a more sustainable energy infrastructure. Another crucial innovation lies in sustainable transportation. The emergence of electric vehicles

(EVs) and advancements in battery technology have ushered in a new era of cleaner, more efficient mobility. Furthermore, the implementation of sustainable urban planning and design principles, such as compact city development, public transit expansion, and pedestrian-friendly infrastructure, is promoting environmentally friendly and socially inclusive transportation systems. Moving beyond energy and transportation, innovations in sustainable agriculture and food production are also making significant strides towards fostering economic sustainability. Techniques such as precision farming, agroecology, vertical farming, and hydroponics are revolutionizing agricultural practices, enabling higher yields with reduced environmental impact. Moreover, advancements in sustainable packaging materials, food waste reduction strategies, and supply chain efficiencies are contributing to the creation of a more sustainable and resilient food system. Furthermore, digital technologies and data analytics play a pivotal role in advancing sustainable economic practices. The utilization of big data, artificial intelligence, and Internet of Things (IoT) sensors enables real-time monitoring and optimization of resource utilization, waste management, and emissions reduction across various industries. This data-driven approach empowers decision-makers to identify opportunities for efficiency improvements and sustainable practices. As demonstrated, these innovative solutions not only offer significant ecological benefits but also present substantial economic opportunities. By fostering sustainable practices and embracing technological innovations, economies can drive long-term growth, create jobs, enhance competitiveness, and secure a more resilient future. However, it is essential to address the barriers to widespread adoption of these innovations, including regulatory frameworks, investment challenges, and public awareness. Overcoming these obstacles will be instrumental in realizing the full potential of sustainable economic practices and ensuring a prosperous and sustainable future for generations to come.

Case Studies of Successful Sustainability Initiatives

In exploring successful sustainability initiatives within the U.S. economic model, it is imperative to delve into real-world examples that have managed to harmonize economic growth with environmental conservation and social responsibility. One such case study revolves around the implementation of renewable energy projects in California. The state has made significant strides in promoting sustainable energy solutions, such as solar and wind power, consequently reducing its dependence on fossil fuels and mitigating carbon emissions. This transition has not only bolstered the state's green economy but has also positioned California as a frontrunner in the global clean energy movement. Another compelling example lies in the realm of corporate sustainability, with industry giants like Patagonia leading the charge. Through their commitment to ethical sourcing, minimization of waste, and advocacy for environmental protection, Patagonia has showcased how aligning business objectives with sustainability principles can yield long-term success while fostering positive impact. Furthermore, the city of Portland, Oregon serves as an exemplar of urban sustainability, pioneering innovative strategies to enhance public transportation, reduce urban sprawl, and promote eco-friendly infrastructure. These diverse case studies underscore the paramount importance of integrating sustainability into various domains of the economy, reinforcing the notion that achieving economic prosperity need not come at the expense of environmental degradation. By scrutinizing these success stories, we gain invaluable insights into the viability and benefits of sustainable practices, inspiring us to reimagine our economic paradigms and embark on a transformative journey towards a more sustainable future.

Proposed Reforms for Economic Sustainability

Economic sustainability is pivotal to the long-term prosperity of any nation, and the United States is no exception. As we navigate through an era of heightened environmental concerns and social inequalities, it becomes increasingly crucial for policymakers and industry leaders to implement reforms that not only address these pressing issues but also ensure the economic well-being of future generations. In this section, we will delve into a comprehensive analysis of proposed reforms that can bolster the economic sustainability of the United States. One of the primary areas of focus is transitioning towards renewable and clean energy sources. A shift away from reliance on fossil fuels not only mitigates ecological harm but also creates opportunities for innovation and job creation. Investing in renewable energy infrastructure, such as solar and wind power, presents a promising avenue for sustainable economic growth. Furthermore, incentivizing industries to adopt eco-friendly practices through tax credits and subsidies can further accelerate the transition to a greener economy. Another critical dimension of economic sustainability revolves around fostering inclusive economic growth. This entails revisiting existing policies to address inequities in wages, healthcare access, and educational opportunities. Proposed reforms may encompass raising the minimum wage, expanding access to affordable healthcare, and implementing tuition-free or subsidized higher education programs. By bolstering the economic security of marginalized communities, the U.S. can cultivate a more resilient and equitable society. Additionally, integrating circular economy principles into manufacturing and consumption patterns can contribute significantly to economic sustainability. Embracing practices that minimize waste generation and promote recycling and reusing resources can reduce the strain on natural ecosystems, while simultaneously creating new economic opportunities. Moreover, incentivizing the development of sustainable technologies and promoting responsible consumption habits aligns with the principles of a circular economy. Finally, a holistic approach to economic sustainability involves regulatory reforms aimed at cultivating transparent and accountable business practices. Strengthening regulations to curb corporate malpractices, promoting ethical investing, and supporting socially responsible enterprises can enhance long-term economic stability. By fostering an environment conducive to ethical business conduct, the U.S. can fortify its economic landscape while upholding core societal values. In conclusion, the proposed reforms presented herein offer a comprehensive framework for advancing economic sustainability in the United States. It is imperative for stakeholders across public and private sectors to collaborate in earnest to actualize these reforms, thereby paving the way for a more prosperous, equitable, and sustainable future.

Political Challenges to Implementing Reforms

Implementing reforms for sustainable economic development is often hindered by political challenges that emerge from differing ideological perspectives, vested interests, and the influence of powerful lobbying groups. One major political challenge to reform is the resistance from entrenched stakeholders who may perceive the proposed changes as a threat to their existing power structures or economic benefits. This opposition can lead to significant hurdles in enacting necessary policy adjustments. Additionally, political polarization and gridlock within legislative bodies can stall or dilute reform efforts, as competing interests struggle to find common ground. Furthermore, the influence of special interest groups and corporate entities on policymakers can impede the implementation of reforms aimed at promoting sustainable economic practices. These influential entities often lobby against policy changes that might undermine their short-term profitability or market dominance, creating barriers to achieving long-term sustainability. Moreover, navigating complex bureaucratic processes and obtaining consensus among diverse political factions can pose substantial challenges for policymakers seeking to usher in comprehensive and effective reforms. The contentious nature of political debates surrounding reform initiatives can lead to protracted negotiations and compromises, potentially resulting in watered-down measures that lack the necessary teeth to drive meaningful change. Another significant political challenge lies in public perception and understanding of the need for reforms. In some cases, lack of public awareness or misconceptions about the potential benefits of sustainable economic practices can undermine support for reform agendas. Additionally, the short-term focus of electoral cycles and political decision-making can inhibit the prioritization of long-term sustainability over immediate economic concerns. Finally, geopolitical dynamics and international relations can introduce complexities in implementing reforms, especially when cross-border economic interests and alliances come into play. As nations strive to balance their domestic economic objectives with global competitiveness, the interplay of political forces at an international level can impact the ability to adopt and enforce sustainable economic policies. Overcoming these political challenges requires strategic coalition-building, transparent communication, and a concerted effort to align divergent interests towards a shared vision of sustainable economic development. It demands innovative approaches to policymaking that address the concerns of various stakeholders while staying committed to the greater goal of fostering an economically and environmentally sustainable future.

Future Perspectives on Sustainable Economic Development

Sustainable economic development entails a comprehensive and integrated approach that prioritizes the long-term health of the economy, society, and the environment. As we look to the future, it is imperative for policymakers, businesses, and individuals to embrace sustainable practices and re-evaluate traditional economic models. The transition towards sustainable economic development presents several potential future perspectives that can shape the trajectory of our global economy.

Firstly, one of the predominant future perspectives revolves around the adoption of circular economy principles. The concept of a circular economy emphasizes minimizing waste and maximizing the use and reusability of resources. This shift in perspective holds the potential to transform industries, reduce environmental degradation, and achieve significant cost savings. Businesses embracing this model may find themselves better positioned for sustained growth while mitigating their ecological footprint.

Secondly, technological innovation is poised to play a pivotal role in shaping sustainable economic development. Advancements in renewable energy, sustainable agriculture, and clean technologies offer promising avenues to decouple economic growth from environmental degradation. Embracing and investing in these technologies is not just an ethical choice; it also presents compelling economic opportunities and job creation prospects.

Furthermore, a future perspective that cannot be overlooked is the increasing awareness and activism surrounding environmental and social issues. The social and environmental consciousness of consumers is progressively influencing market dynamics and corporate behavior. This evolving landscape calls for greater transparency, accountability, and responsible governance in business practices. As such, organizations that proactively align their strategies with sustainable development goals stand to gain competitive advantages and bolster their reputations.

Another crucial aspect of future perspectives on sustainable economic development involves international collaboration and partnerships. Given the interconnectedness of the global economy, collective action on a multinational scale is essential. Collaborative efforts could involve sharing best practices, aligning regulations, and leveraging financial resources to support developing nations in their pursuit of sustainable development. International cooperation will be imperative in addressing complex challenges such as climate change, resource depletion, and poverty alleviation.

Looking ahead, the promotion of sustainable economic development demands a holistic paradigm shift – one that transcends short-term gains and requires a redefinition of success. It necessitates a concerted effort to balance economic prosperity with ecological sustainability and social equity. Embracing these future perspectives offers the promise of creating resilient economies that thrive within the planetary boundaries, uphold societal well-being, and foster intergenerational equity.

CORPORATE INFLUENCE ON U.S. ECONOMIC POLICY

INTRODUCTION TO CORPORATE POWER AND POLICY INFLUENCE

The historical relationship between corporate power and policy influence in the United States is a compelling narrative that has profoundly shaped the country's economic landscape. For decades, corporations have exerted significant influence on U.S. legislation, leveraging their resources, networks, and lobbying capabilities to effectively shape economic decisions at a national level. The intertwining of corporate interests with government policymaking reflects a foundational aspect of the American economic system. Understanding this dynamic is paramount to comprehending the forces that drive the nation's economic policies and regulatory framework. Corporate entities hold considerable sway due to their substantial economic footprint, which encompasses employment, investments, and contributions to GDP. Consequently, their interactions with federal and state governments play a pivotal role in shaping economic regulations, tax codes, and trade policies. Furthermore, the impacts of corporate influence extend beyond specific industries, permeating every facet of the national economy. The continuous interplay between policymakers and corporate stakeholders has cultivated an environment where economic decisions are intricately intertwined with the interests of the private sector. Furthermore, as globalization and technological advancements have expanded the reach of corporations, their influence over U.S. economic policies has become more pervasive and complex. As such, examining the historical underpinnings of corporate power and its policy influence provides invaluable insights into the mechanisms that steer the nation's economic decision-making processes.

Historical Overview of Corporate Impact on U.S. Legislation

The historical influence of corporations on U.S. legislation dates back to the early years of the nation's formation. From the Gilded Age to the present day, corporate interests have played a significant role in shaping economic and regulatory policies. During the late 19th and early 20th centuries, powerful industrialists such as Andrew Carnegie, John D. Rockefeller, and J.P. Morgan amassed immense wealth and utilized their financial resources to sway government decision-making. This era witnessed the rise of monopolies and trusts, prompting concerns about the concentration of economic power in the hands of a few influential figures. As a result, legislative measures like the Sherman Antitrust Act were enacted to curb monopolistic practices. However, despite these efforts, corporate influence continued to permeate legislative corridors. The post-World War II period saw the emergence of large multinational corporations wielding substantial political clout. The Cold War context further intertwined corporate interests with national security and foreign policy goals. Throughout this phase, the military-industrial complex gained prominence, leading to heightened corporate involvement in defense-related legislation and procurement. Additionally, the proliferation of industry-specific lobbying organizations and political action committees consolidated corporate power and paved the way for targeted advocacy and campaign contributions. Notably, landmark events such as the Watergate scandal highlighted the nexus between corporate contributions and political decision-making, catalyzing public demands for transparency and ethical governance. Subsequent legislative responses, including campaign finance reforms and lobbying disclosure requirements, sought to address concerns surrounding undue corporate influence. Nonetheless, the evolution of corporate structures and the expansion of global commerce presented new challenges in navigating the intricate dynamics of corporate influence on U.S. legislation. In the contemporary landscape, the intersection of economic policy, corporate advocacy, and technological advancements continues to redefine the boundaries of corporate impact on legislative processes. Thus, an examination of historical precedents illuminates the enduring saga of corporate influence on U.S. legislation, underscoring the intricate interplay between economic imperatives, political dynamics, and societal welfare.

Analysis of Corporate Lobbying in U.S. Economic Policy Formation

Corporate lobbying has been a pervasive force in shaping U.S. economic policy, exerting influence through various channels to advance the interests of business entities. The corridors of power in Washington D.C. are often inundated with lobbyists representing corporations seeking favorable policies and regulations that align with their objectives. This practice has been deeply entrenched in the U.S. political landscape, raising critical questions about the balance of power and representation within the policymaking process.

The intricate nature of corporate lobbying involves extensive interactions between industry representatives and policymakers. Through direct advocacy, campaign contributions, and participation in advisory committees, corporations leverage their resources to mold economic legislation in ways that serve their commercial goals. While lobbying itself is a legitimate means of petitioning the government, concerns arise when it disproportionately influences decision-making, potentially tilting the scale in favor of narrow corporate interests at the expense of broader societal welfare.

Moreover, the breadth and depth of corporate lobbying extend beyond mere persuasion, encompassing sophisticated strategies mobilized to shape public opinion and sway policy outcomes. By engaging in astute public relations campaigns, funding think tanks, and supporting research that aligns with their positions, corporations strategically maneuver to build narratives that resonate with policymakers and the public. This multifaceted approach amplifies the impact of corporate influence, permeating the discourse surrounding economic policies and regulatory frameworks.

At the core of the analysis of corporate lobbying lies the ethical considerations intertwined with the pursuit of business objectives. The sheer magnitude of financial resources allocated to lobbying activities raises pertinent questions about equity, fairness, and transparency in the policymaking process. Concerns regarding the potential distortion of democratic ideals, unequal access to decision-makers, and the prevalence of regulatory capture prompt a critical evaluation of the existing mechanisms governing corporate influence.

Furthermore, assessing the implications of corporate lobbying necessitates an exploration of its effects on economic stability, market competition, and consumer welfare. The alignment of economic policies with corporate preferences can wield substantial ramifications, influencing market dynamics, income distribution, and the overall resilience of the economic system. Such a convergence underscores the imperative need for a comprehensive understanding of the intricate interplay between corporate influence and the formulation of U.S. economic policies.

In essence, the analysis of corporate lobbying in U.S. economic policy formation calls for a discerning evaluation of its ethical, political, and socioeconomic dimensions. Recognizing the far-reaching implications of corporate influence on the policy landscape underscores the importance of fostering transparency, accountability, and inclusivity in the decision-making processes that underpin the nation's economic governance.

The Effect of Tax Policies on Corporate Behavior and Economic Stability

Tax policies play a pivotal role in shaping corporate behavior and maintaining economic stability within the United States. At the most fundamental level, tax laws influence how corporations allocate resources, make investment decisions, and engage in business activities. By examining the direct and indirect implications of tax policies, we can gain insight into their profound impact on the broader economic landscape. One of the primary effects of tax policies is their influence on corporations' capital allocation strategies. Favorable tax treatment for specific investments or activities can incentivize corporations to direct their resources towards those areas, potentially stimulating growth and innovation in particular sectors. Conversely, punitive tax measures may dissuade corporations from pursuing certain ventures, leading to a reallocation of capital and potential shifts in industry dynamics. Furthermore, tax policies can significantly affect corporate financial planning and decision-making. The ability to deduct expenses, access tax credits, or navigate international tax structures can heavily impact a corporation's bottom line and its propensity to engage in various financial activities. Tax incentives for research and development, for instance, can spur innovation and technological advancement, while tax burdens related to overseas operations can sway companies' global business strategies. In considering the broader economic stability, tax policies also hold substantial weight. Through fiscal and monetary mechanisms, taxes serve as critical tools for government revenue generation and economic regulation. By adjusting tax rates, deductions, and credits, policymakers can influence consumer spending, investment patterns, and overall market conditions. Moreover, tax policies are closely tied to public welfare programs, infrastructure development, and social services, all of which contribute to the stability and well-being of the nation. However, achieving an optimal balance between corporate interests and broader economic stability is paramount. Excessive corporate tax breaks, loopholes, or preferential treatment can lead to growing income inequality, diminished public resources, and economic distortions. Conversely, overly burdensome corporate tax regimes could stifle business activity, hinder competitiveness, and undermine economic growth. Striking the right equilibrium in tax policy design requires a nuanced understanding of corporate dynamics, economic interdependencies, and societal needs. It demands a comprehensive examination of the short- and long-term ramifications of tax adjustments on corporate behavior, economic stability, and national prosperity.

Corporate Influence on Military Spending

The allocation of military spending is a critical component of a nation's economic policy, and in the United States, it has long been influenced by corporate interests. The relationship between corporations and military spending dates back to the early stages of the military-industrial complex, where defense contractors and other entities involved in national security have wielded significant influence over government decisions regarding defense expenditure. This influence extends through lobbying efforts, campaign contributions, and strategic partnerships that shape the prioritization of defense projects and programs. As a result, the allocation of military funds may not always align with the genuine strategic and security needs of the nation, but rather with the vested interests of corporate entities within the defense industry.

The impact of corporate influence on military spending can be observed in various aspects, including the procurement of weapons systems, development of military technology, and deployment of personnel. Defense contractors often seek to promote and sustain programs that are financially advantageous to their organizations, leading to the perpetuation of certain weapon platforms or technologies that may not be the most cost-effective or strategically optimal choices. Furthermore, the revolving door between the government and defense industry allows for key decision-makers to transition between public office and lucrative private sector positions, creating potential conflicts of interest and further entrenching corporate influence within the military establishment.

Moreover, the extent of corporate influence on military spending also raises ethical considerations. Decision-making processes related to defense allocations should prioritize national security imperatives, efficiency, and public interest over the profit motives of individual corporations. There is a need for transparency and accountability in ensuring that military expenditures are directed towards enhancing the country's defense capabilities rather than merely serving commercial interests. Furthermore, the influence of corporations on military spending can potentially lead to an overemphasis on certain types of military capabilities while neglecting other essential areas such as cybersecurity, intelligence, and asymmetric warfare tactics.

As we navigate the complexities of corporate influence on military spending, it is crucial to evaluate the mechanisms through which this influence operates and consider reforms that can mitigate undue corporate sway over defense allocations. By fostering a more balanced and transparent decision-making framework, policymakers can uphold the integrity of military budgeting and ensure that national security remains the paramount objective. Moreover, promoting competition, encouraging innovation, and diversifying procurement sources can help counteract the monopolistic tendencies that arise from excessive corporate influence. Ultimately, a comprehensive reassessment of the relationship between corporations and military spending is imperative to safeguard the integrity and efficiency of the nation's defense infrastructure.

Case Studies: Major Corporations and Their Role in Policy Making

The influence of major corporations on policy making in the United States has been a subject of intense scrutiny and debate.

Examining case studies provides valuable insights into how corporate interests shape economic policy and regulation. One prominent case is that of the pharmaceutical industry, which has invested significant resources in lobbying for favorable legislation and regulations related to drug pricing, patents, and clinical trials. The ability of pharmaceutical companies to influence lawmakers through campaign contributions, professional advocacy, and direct lobbying activities has resulted in policies that protect their profitability.

Another compelling example is the role of technology giants in shaping internet privacy laws and data protection regulations. Companies like Facebook, Google, and Amazon have actively engaged with policymakers to influence the development of legislation relating to user data, online advertising, and antitrust issues. Their significant economic power has allowed them to shape the discourse surrounding digital privacy and competition policy, often to their advantage.

Furthermore, the energy sector, particularly oil and gas companies, has played a pivotal role in influencing environmental regulations and energy policies. Through strategic alliances with influential legislators, targeted public relations campaigns, and substantial financial contributions, these companies have influenced policies governing carbon emissions, offshore drilling, and renewable energy incentives, often to the detriment of environmental sustainability.

In addition to these specific cases, the role of major financial institutions in crafting regulatory frameworks and fiscal policies cannot be overlooked. Banks, investment firms, and insurance companies wield considerable influence over legislation related to banking regulations, tax reforms, and consumer protections. Case studies focusing on the involvement of Wall Street in shaping financial policies reveal the intricate connections between corporate interests, government decision-making, and economic outcomes.

Analyzing these case studies not only underscores the pervasive influence of major corporations on policy making but also raises critical questions about the balance between corporate power and the public interest. It prompts a deeper reflection on the ethical implications of regulatory capture, the concentration of economic influence, and the need for greater transparency and accountability in the policymaking process.

Policy Shifts: Observing Changes in Economic Norms Due to Corporate Advocacy

Policies and economic norms are deeply interconnected, often shaped through a complex interplay of political, social, and corporate influences. The sphere of corporate advocacy holds significant sway over policy formation, and its impact on economic norms cannot be overstated. In observing the historical trajectory of economic policymaking, one can discern the tangible imprints left by corporate advocacy through policy shifts and normative changes.

The process of policy formulation is subject to continuous influence from various stakeholders, including major corporations, industry lobbies, and special interest groups. These influencers strategically navigate the corridors of power, leveraging their resources, connections, and expertise to shape legislation that aligns with their objectives. Such assertive involvement often results in observable shifts in economic norms, as policies are recalibrated to accommodate corporate interests.

Corporate advocacy has engendered notable shifts in economic norms, often redefining the boundaries of regulation, taxation, and market dynamics. This has led to the relaxation or reinforcement of regulatory frameworks, alterations in tax structures, and modifications in market competition dynamics. As a consequence, these shifts have ushered in a new era of economic norms, reshaping the landscape within which businesses operate and citizens interact with financial systems.

Moreover, the impact of corporate advocacy on economic norms extends beyond the legislative sphere, permeating public discourse and shaping societal attitudes towards fiscal and regulatory matters. Through strategic messaging and public relations efforts, corporations position themselves as drivers of economic growth and prosperity, influencing public perception and normalizing certain economic practices. This normalization, in turn, breeds acceptance of policy shifts that align with corporate interests, ultimately embedding these changes into the fabric of the economy.

As we dissect the nuanced interplay between corporate advocacy and economic norms, it becomes evident that these policy shifts not only reflect an evolving regulatory landscape, but also mirror the intricate power dynamics at play within contemporary societies. Recognizing and analyzing these shifts is therefore imperative in gauging the true extent of corporate influence on economic policies and norms. Ultimately, understanding the driving forces behind policy shifts can elucidate the broader implications for the economy, governance structures, and societal well-being, providing critical insights for future policymaking endeavors.

Balancing Corporate Interests with Public Good

As we navigate the intricate landscape of economic policy, it becomes increasingly paramount to address the equilibrium between corporate interests and the public good. Striking a delicate balance between these two entities is essential for fostering a thriving and equitable society. Incorporating the perspectives of various stakeholders, including government representatives, business leaders, economists, and advocacy groups, is crucial in formulating policies that harmonize corporate goals with the welfare of the general populace. A fundamental aspect of this equilibrium involves the implementation of regulations and oversight mechanisms to ensure that corporate activities are conducted in a manner that upholds societal well-being. Through transparent and accountable governance, we can mitigate the potential adverse effects of unchecked corporate influence while preserving the entrepreneurial spirit and innovation that drive economic growth.

Furthermore, an emphasis on corporate social responsibility (CSR) is instrumental in aligning business objectives with broader societal interests. Encouraging corporate entities to engage in ethical practices, sustainable operations, and community investment can contribute to the advancement of public welfare while promoting long-term business success. This approach fosters a mutually beneficial relationship wherein corporations thrive within a supportive societal framework, while simultaneously enhancing the overall quality of life for the citizenry. Moreover, incentivizing responsible corporate behavior through tax credits, subsidies, and public recognition can serve as a powerful method for steering businesses towards activities that generate positive externalities and uphold public values.

Balancing corporate interests with public good also necessitates a comprehensive examination of economic externalities, ensuring that corporate pursuits do not result in detrimental social or environmental consequences. Implementing regulations that internalize external costs, such as pollution and resource depletion, incentivizes corporations to adopt sustainable and environmentally conscious practices. Additionally, fostering dialogue between industry leaders and environmental experts can facilitate the development of innovative strategies that reconcile business imperatives with ecological preservation. By constructing a regulatory ecosystem that rewards companies for minimizing negative externalities and advancing societal well-being, we can align corporate pursuits with the promotion of public good.

Ultimately, achieving a harmonious equilibrium between corporate interests and public welfare demands a multifaceted approach. Through collaborative efforts, inclusive policymaking, and conscientious stewardship, we can forge an economic landscape where corporations contribute to the prosperity and advancement of society at large. Embracing transparency, accountability, and stakeholder engagement lays the groundwork for a sustainable and equitable relationship between corporations and the public good, nurturing a socio-economic environment characterized by shared prosperity and collective progress.

Future Implications of Continued Corporate Influence

The future implications of continued corporate influence on U.S. economic policy are profound and far-reaching. As corporations continue to wield significant power in shaping policy decisions, there are several potential scenarios that could unfold, each with its own implications for the economy, governance, and society as a whole. One possible outcome is the further consolidation of corporate power, leading to increased inequality and a diminished voice for the broader public. This scenario could see policies increasingly skewed towards benefiting the interests of large corporations at the expense of smaller businesses and individual citizens. Moreover, unchecked corporate influence may erode the regulatory framework designed to safeguard against monopolistic behavior, potentially resulting in reduced competition and innovation. Another concerning implication is the potential distortion of public priorities. As corporate interests continue to hold sway over policy-making processes, there is a risk that societal needs and concerns take a backseat to the agenda of powerful corporate entities. This could lead to a widening gap between the policies enacted and the actual needs of the population. Furthermore, the ongoing influence of corporations on economic policy may perpetuate environmental degradation and unsustainable practices, as profit motives often conflict with long-term ecological considerations. However, it is important to note that there are also opportunities for positive change. With heightened awareness of the implications of corporate influence, there is potential for greater public scrutiny and demands for transparency. Efforts to curb undue corporate influence and promote a more equitable policy-making process may gain momentum, leading to reforms aimed at rebalancing the scales between corporate interests and the public good. Additionally, emerging models of corporate social responsibility and sustainable business practices have the potential to guide a shift towards more responsible and inclusive economic policies. Ultimately, the future implications of corporate influence on U.S. economic policy will depend on the interplay of various factors, including public engagement, regulatory responses, and evolving corporate behaviors. Recognizing these implications is crucial for informed decision-making and charting a path towards a more balanced and equitable economic landscape.

Summary and Reflection on Corporate Power in U.S. Economic Policy

The influence of corporations on the formation of U.S. economic policy has been a subject of ongoing debate and scrutiny. As we reflect on the extensive analysis conducted in this book, it becomes evident that corporate power is deeply entrenched in the decision-making processes that shape economic policy in the United States. This summary aims to synthesize the key insights and implications brought forth through the exploration of corporate influence on U.S. economic policy.

Throughout history, corporations have strategically leveraged their resources and influence to shape legislative agendas and regulatory frameworks that align with their interests. From wielding substantial lobbying power to actively participating in the drafting of policies, corporations have been instrumental in influencing tax policies, trade regulations, and government spending. The pervasive nature of corporate influence raises critical questions about the balance between private sector interests and the public good.

Examining the future implications of continued corporate influence reveals potential challenges and opportunities. The evolving landscape of technology, globalization, and environmental sustainability introduces complex dynamics that further intertwine corporate interests with national economic priorities. As such, policymakers and stakeholders must critically evaluate the long-term effects of existing corporate influence and explore avenues for promoting greater accountability, transparency, and ethical conduct within corporate advocacy.

Moreover, this reflection underscores the need for comprehensive reform and proactive measures to mitigate the adverse effects of unbridled corporate power. Addressing the socio-economic disparities and systemic inequities perpetuated by undue corporate influence requires a multi-faceted approach that engages diverse perspectives and expertise. By fostering constructive dialogue and collaborative partnerships, society can strive towards revitalizing democratic principles and restoring a fair and balanced policy-making framework that prioritizes the collective welfare.

In conclusion, the intricate relationship between corporate power and U.S. economic policy necessitates continued vigilance and informed discourse. By acknowledging the complexities of corporate influence and championing responsible governance, we can endeavor to forge an economic landscape that upholds integrity, fosters innovation, and serves the best interests of both corporate entities and the broader community.

CONCLUSION: A NEW WORLD ORDER?

OVERVIEW OF PRINCIPAL DISCUSSIONS

The journey through this book has presented an intricate tapestry of insights and observations, culminating in a profound understanding of the shifting global economic landscape. Within the discourse on China's economic transformation, we delved into the historical context that underpins its evolution, elucidating the drivers of its remarkable poverty reduction and sustained growth. This was juxtaposed against the U.S. economic trajectory, with a careful examination of the 2008 financial crisis and the intricate web of interdependence between these two economic powerhouses. Moreover, the rise of BRICS was analyzed, offering a broader perspective on the shifting dynamics of economic influence. In the U.S. context, sustainability issues and corporate influence on economic policy were scrutinized, providing valuable insights into the complexities shaping its economic model. Each chapter acted as a lens, focusing on distinct yet interconnected facets of the global order. The synthesis of China's ascendancy and U.S. challenges emerged as a recurring motif, weaving through the narrative, highlighting the seismic shifts underway in the geo-economic arena. The convergence of these discussions underscores the emergent multipolar world, fraught with opportunities and vulnerabilities. As we navigate through the intricacies of global economic leadership, the confluence of these principal discussions presents a compelling tableau of the complex interplay between nations, economies, and policies. This overview sets the stage for a deeper exploration of the synergies and tensions shaping the contours of the ever-evolving new world order.

Synthesis of China's Ascendancy and U.S. Challenges

China's economic ascendancy has been a focal point in the global arena, sparking intense discussions and debates concerning its implications for the United States and the existing global order. For decades, the U.S. stood as the uncontested superpower, shaping international relations and playing a dominant role in global economic governance. However, the dramatic rise of China has disrupted this long-standing status quo, presenting a multitude of complex challenges for the U.S. and the world at large.

At the heart of China's ascendancy lies its rapid economic growth, driven by an unprecedented wave of industrialization and urbanization. This expansion has propelled China to the forefront of the global economy, challenging the established dominance of the U.S. and creating a new economic landscape. The sheer scale and pace of China's growth have reshaped international trade patterns, investment flows, and technological innovation, leading to a reconfiguration of global economic power dynamics.

Concurrently, the U.S. faces a range of formidable challenges that are intertwined with China's ascent. These challenges encompass economic, geopolitical, and strategic dimensions, precipitated by China's growing influence and assertiveness on the world stage. From the ballooning trade deficit to the thorny issues of intellectual property theft and technology transfer, the U.S. is grappling with the ramifications of China's economic prowess. Moreover, the changing dynamics of global politics, with China seeking to expand its sphere of influence, pose a direct challenge to traditional U.S. hegemony.

The synthesis of China's ascendancy and U.S. challenges necessitates a comprehensive understanding of the interlinkages between the two economic powerhouses. This synthesis entails examining the intricate web of economic interdependence, geopolitical rivalries, and strategic maneuvering that underpin their interactions. Furthermore, it requires a nuanced evaluation of the policy responses and strategies adopted by each nation to navigate this shifting paradigm of global economic power.

In light of these complex dynamics, it becomes imperative to delve into the strategic choices before the U.S. - whether to cooperate, compete, or confront China's ascendancy. Each option carries profound implications for the future trajectory of global economic governance, trade relations, and the quest for international stability. Crafting effective strategies to address these challenges demands astute diplomatic acumen, foresight, and a keen appreciation of the multifaceted nature of Sino-U.S. relations.

Ultimately, the synthesis of China's ascendancy and U.S. challenges embodies a pivotal juncture in the annals of global economics, serving as a compelling narrative that unfolds against the backdrop of an evolving international order.

The Paradigm Shift in Global Economic Power

As China's economic influence continues to ascend and the United States faces significant challenges, the world is witnessing a profound paradigm shift in global economic power. This shift is fundamentally altering the dynamics of international trade, investment, and geopolitical relationships. The traditional dominance of Western economies, particularly the U.S., is being recalibrated against the backdrop of China's remarkable rise as a global economic powerhouse.

At the core of this paradigm shift is the reconfiguration of global supply chains, production networks, and economic interdependencies. China's emergence as a key player in these domains has introduced new dimensions to global economic architecture, challenging established norms and reshaping the contours of international commerce. The Belt and Road Initiative, for instance, illustrates China's ambitious vision to enhance connectivity and infrastructure across continents, signaling its proactive role in shaping the global economic landscape.

Moreover, the paradigm shift manifests in the evolving nature of economic alliances and multilateral frameworks. Traditional forums such as the G7 are confronting the need to adapt to an era where emerging economies like China are assuming greater influence and leadership roles. This signifies a significant departure from historical power structures and necessitates a recalibration of international institutions to reflect the changing distribution of economic power.

Furthermore, this paradigm shift entails a reevaluation of economic sovereignty and technological prowess. With China's rapid advancements in areas such as artificial intelligence, renewable energy, and digital commerce, there is a discernible rebalancing of innovation and industrial capabilities on a global scale. The implications of this reorientation extend beyond economic realms and have far-reaching geopolitical ramifications, influencing strategic partnerships and competition among nations.

In essence, the paradigm shift in global economic power underscores the imperative for stakeholders to accommodate the dynamics of a multipolar world order. As the contours of economic dominance undergo transformation, strategic foresight and adaptive policies will be essential for navigating this terrain. By understanding the shifts in global economic power, nations can proactively engage with emerging trends, foster collaborative frameworks, and contribute to the collective design of a balanced and equitable global economic order.

Forecasting the Geo-Economic Landscape

The geo-economic landscape of the world is undergoing a profound transformation, driven by the rise of emerging economies and the reconfiguration of global trade patterns. In forecasting this evolving terrain, it is imperative to consider a multitude of factors that encompass economic, geopolitical, technological, and environmental dimensions. One key aspect is the realignment of economic power, with indicators pointing towards a shift from a unipolar world dominated by the United States to a multipolar system where China, alongside other emerging powers, assumes a central role. This suggests a reconfiguration of global economic governance and ushering in an era of increased cooperation and competition among diverse stakeholders. Another critical consideration is the impact of technological advancements on the geo-economic landscape. The rapid proliferation of disruptive technologies such as artificial intelligence, blockchain, and renewable energy solutions is reshaping traditional economic structures and altering the competitive dynamics between nations. Moreover, the escalating urgency of climate change and environmental sustainability presents a pivotal factor in forecasting the geo-economic landscape. As countries adapt to a low-carbon future, renewable energy, sustainable infrastructure, and innovative environmental policies will increasingly influence economic competitiveness and global trade relationships. The interplay of geopolitical dynamics further complicates the forecast, with issues such as trade tensions, territorial disputes, and strategic alliances shaping the contours of the future geo-economic landscape. Moreover, the evolving nature of international institutions and regional blocs contributes to the complexity of such forecasting, warranting an awareness of how these entities influence economic integration and global power dynamics. Additionally, analyzing demographic shifts, urbanization trends, and migration patterns is crucial in predicting the spatial distribution of economic activity and the emergence of new economic hubs. Understanding these multifaceted factors and their interconnections is essential for effectively forecasting the evolving geo-economic landscape, enabling policymakers, businesses, and individuals to anticipate and adapt to the complexities of the future global economy.

Scenarios for Future Economic Preeminence

The future economic preeminence of nations rests upon a complex interplay of factors, from demographic shifts to technological innovation, and geopolitical realignments. While traditional economic powerhouses like the United States have long dominated the global economic landscape, the rise of emerging economies like China, India, and Brazil has introduced new variables and uncertainties. In this context, forecasting scenarios for future economic preeminence necessitates a nuanced understanding of historical precedent, current trends, and potential disruptions. One scenario involves the continuation of the status quo, where existing powers maintain their dominance through incremental adjustments to policies and strategies. Alternatively, a multipolar world could emerge, with multiple economic superpowers operating on more equal footing, albeit with heightened competition and cooperation dynamics. Another prospect involves the ascent of a new singular economic powerhouse, potentially propelled by breakthroughs in technology, resource abundance, or other transformative catalysts. Conversely, a deglobalization scenario unfolds, characterized by fragmentation of trade blocs, protectionist policies, and regional economic silos. Each scenario carries diverse implications for both developed and developing economies, reshaping global supply chains, investment patterns, and geopolitical alliances. Adapting to these potential futures requires foresight, agility, and collaborative diplomacy. It demands that governments, businesses, and international organizations anticipate and navigate evolving macroeconomic landscapes, embracing innovation, sustainable development, and inclusive growth strategies. Moreover, it calls for proactive measures to address geopolitical tensions, foster cross-border dialogue, and construct resilient institutional frameworks. As we explore these scenarios, it becomes evident that the trajectory of future economic preeminence is not predetermined; instead, it hinges on the informed choices and coordinated actions of global stakeholders. By unpacking and critically assessing these potential paths, societies can proactively shape a more stable, prosperous, and equitable global economic order.

Global Political Dynamics and Economic Leadership

In the context of the shifting global economic landscape, the interface between political dynamics and economic leadership plays a pivotal role in defining the trajectory of nations and international relations. As economic power diffuses across diverse regions, political actors are compelled to recalibrate their geopolitical strategies to maintain influence and relevance on the world stage. The rise of emerging economies, particularly China, and the continued dominance of established powers create a complex web of interdependencies that require astute navigation.

At the heart of these global political dynamics lies the question of economic leadership—both in terms of stewardship within individual nations and collective cooperation on a global scale. The extents to which nations leverage their economic prowess to assert political primacy shape the contours of contemporary geopolitics. China's ascendant economic status and its parallel efforts to exercise commensurate political influence demonstrate the inseparable link between economic might and global leadership.

Amid this landscape, it becomes imperative to dissect the power dynamics at play and examine the varying models of economic leadership. The contrast between China's state-directed economic model and the market-driven principles embraced by the United States underscores the divergent approaches to economic governance and their implications for global political dynamics. Furthermore, the evolving roles played by international financial institutions and multilateral arrangements bring forth questions about equitable representation and decision-making structures in the international economic order.

The interplay between economic heft and diplomatic maneuvering underscores the salient point that economic leadership is intrinsic to fostering stability, prosperity, and cooperation at a global level. Moreover, as aspirations for sustainable development and inclusive growth take center stage, a reexamination of economic leadership necessitates an analysis of its impact on sociopolitical stability and the broader quest for international harmony. Through a nuanced understanding of global political dynamics and economic leadership, nations can chart courses for constructive engagement and collaborative problem-solving, paving the way for a more equitable and resilient global order.

Economic Policy and International Stability

The nexus between economic policy and international stability is a critical consideration as the global economy grapples with evolving challenges. International stability is contingent on the economic policies pursued by nations, which directly influence global dynamics. It is imperative to recognize that economic policy decisions have far-reaching implications on not only domestic economies but also on the interconnectedness of the global economic landscape. As such, policymakers must carefully deliberate and implement economic measures with a keen eye on fostering international stability. One of the primary aspects in this regard is the coordination of fiscal and monetary policies among nations to mitigate systemic risks and ensure global economic equilibrium. By aligning economic policies to promote stability, countries contribute to sustainable growth and resilience in the face of economic shocks. Furthermore, engaging in diplomatic relations to understand and address potential conflicts arising from economic policy disparities is paramount. These efforts are pivotal for upholding stable international relations and preventing economic discord that can exacerbate global instability. The continuity of free and fair trade practices, combined with transparent regulatory frameworks, plays a pivotal role in fostering international stability. Furthermore, embracing multilateralism and cooperation through international institutions is essential to address shared challenges and foster collective prosperity. Striving to establish resilient and inclusive economic policies will contribute to global stability, providing a solid foundation for sustained international cooperation. In conclusion, the intertwining of economic policy and international stability underscores the need for astute and collaborative measures to navigate the intricacies of the global economy. By prioritizing stability and fostering inclusive economic policies at the international level, nations can fortify the foundations of a more stable and prosperous world.

Corporate Influence Revisited

Corporate influence on global economic affairs has been a subject of intense scrutiny and debate in recent decades. The interplay between multinational corporations and sovereign nations continues to shape the trajectory of the international economic order. In revisiting corporate influence, it is imperative to critically examine the evolving roles and responsibilities of corporations within the context of a shifting global landscape.

The contemporary era has seen an unprecedented rise in the scale and scope of multinational corporations, with these entities exerting substantial economic sway and often traversing geographical boundaries in their quest for market dominance. This expansion has prompted concerns about the potential for undue influence on policymaking, strategic resource allocation, and economic regulations at both national and supranational levels.

Moving Towards a Multipolar World

As we navigate the complex fabric of global geopolitics, one cannot overlook the palpable shift towards a multipolar world. The traditional hegemony of a singular superpower is being challenged by the emergence of multiple centers of influence, each with its own sphere of economic, political, and cultural sway. This ongoing transformation has significant implications for international relations, fostering a more diverse and inter-connected global landscape where power is decentralized and multi-dimensional.

The rise of China as an economic powerhouse, coupled with the steadfast resilience of the United States, along with the re-surgence of Russia and the collective influence of the European Union, signals the dawn of a multipolar era. This geopolitical re-configuration introduces a new dynamic into the international arena, reshaping diplomatic alliances, trade relations, and stra-tegic partnerships. As the world transitions away from a uni-polar dominance, new avenues for collaboration and competition emerge, fundamentally altering the traditional dynamics of global governance.

In this evolving milieu, the concept of multipolarity infuses a sense of equilibrium, as diverse actors engage in shaping the contours of a new international order. Nations are compelled to navigate this intricate web of intersecting interests and divergent ideologies, as they seek to assert their influence on the global stage. Moreover, the multipolar framework demands a reevalua-tion of traditional power structures, instigating a reconfiguration of global institutions and norms to accommodate the burgeoning plurality of influential actors.

Furthermore, the proliferation of multipolarity engenders a paradigm shift in the conduct of international diplomacy and economic interdependence. It necessitates a recalibration of strategies governing trade, investment, and development initiatives, as countries navigate this convoluted web of multifaceted relationships. Cross-regional cooperation, multilateral agreements, and economic integration have become pivotal instruments in managing the complexities of a multipolar world, heralding a new chapter in global economic and political interactions.

As we traverse this transition, the trajectory of a multipolar world prompts a reassessment of national interests and collective aspirations. Nations grapple with aligning their policies within an intricate tapestry of interwoven objectives, seeking to harness the potential for mutual benefit amidst competitive dynamics. This era of multipolarity embodies both the promise of collaborative synergy and the challenges of managing divergent narratives, forging a narrative of coexistence and competition that underpins the global trajectory of the 21st century.

Strategic Directions for Sustained International Cooperation

In the contemporary global landscape, the need for sustained international cooperation has become paramount. As the world transitions towards a multipolar reality with a shifting balance of power, strategic directions must be charted to ensure stability, prosperity, and harmony among nations. The concept of sustained international cooperation transcends traditional alliances and geopolitical agendas, encompassing economic interdependence, shared security imperatives, and collaborative efforts towards addressing transnational challenges. To achieve this ambitious objective, several strategic directions can be envisaged. Firstly, there is a pressing need to strengthen the existing multilateral frameworks such as the United Nations, World Trade Organization, and regional organizations like the European Union and

African Union. These institutions play a crucial role in fostering dialogue, resolving disputes, and promoting cooperation on a wide spectrum of issues ranging from trade and investment to peacekeeping and humanitarian assistance. Secondly, a renewed emphasis on diplomacy and conflict resolution mechanisms is imperative. Effective channels for dialogue and negotiation, coupled with mediation and arbitration measures, can mitigate interstate tensions and prevent conflicts from escalating into full-scale confrontations. Moreover, investing in preventive diplomacy and early warning systems can pre-empt potential crises and allow for timely interventions. Thirdly, the promotion of economic interconnectedness and development-oriented partnerships is vital. By bolstering international trade, investment, and infrastructure collaboration, nations can harness their respective comparative advantages for mutual benefit. This necessitates a re-evaluation of global supply chains, digital connectivity, and sustainable development initiatives to foster inclusive growth and poverty alleviation. Furthermore, embracing technological innovation and knowledge transfer can foster cross-border synergies, while initiatives such as the Belt and Road Initiative exemplify the potential for mutually beneficial economic cooperation. Fourthly, a concerted effort towards environmental stewardship and climate action is indispensable for sustained international cooperation. Addressing climate change, natural disasters, and resource management demands collective action and shared responsibility. Collaborative research and technology exchange in renewable energy, ecological conservation, and disaster resilience can fortify global resilience and safeguard the planet for future generations. Fifthly, upholding universal human rights, inclusivity, and cultural diversity underpin the ethical dimensions of sustained international cooperation. Respect for human dignity, social justice, and gender equality must be embedded in all cooperative endeavors to forge a truly harmonious world order. This entails championing education, intercultural dialogue, and cultural exchange programs that foster mutual understanding and respect. Additionally, the preservation of indigenous knowledge, languages, and heritage contributes to the richness and diversity of humankind. In conclusion, the strategic directions for sustained international cooperation outlined above are instrumental in navigating the complexities of an increasingly interdependent and multipolar world. Embracing these directions requires visionary leadership, unwavering commitment, and a collective will to transcend transient interests in favor of a more equitable, secure, and prosperous global community.